ACTS

OF THE

GENERAL ASSEMBLY

OF THE

STATE OF VIRGINIA.

PASSED AT THE

EXTRA SESSION,

Commenced December 4, 1862, in the 87th year of the Commonwealth.

WHEELING:

JOHN F. M'DERMOT, PUBLIC PRINTER.

1863.

ACTS OF THE GENERAL ASSEMBLY,

PASSED AT THE EXTRA SESSION COMMENCED DEC. 4, 1862.

CHAP. 1.—An ACT for the relief of John Slack, Jr., Sheriff elect of Kanawha County.

Passed December 13, 1862

1. Be it enacted by the General Assembly, That John Slack, jr., Sheriff elect of Kanawha county, be allowed until the twentieth day of February, one thousand eight hundred and sixty-three, to give bond and qualify as Sheriff of said county.

2. This act shall be in force from its passage.

John Slack, Jr., Sheriff elect of Kanawha county allowed until the 20th day of February, 1863 to give bond and qualify as Sheriff of said county.
Commencement.

CHAP. 2.—An ACT to amend the 5th section of an Act entitled an Act to incorporate the City of Wheeling, in Ohio County.

Passed December 19, 1862.

1. Be it enacted by the General Assembly, That section 5th of an Act entitled "an Act to incorporate the city of Wheeling, in Ohio county, passed March 11th, 1836," be amended and re-enacted so as to read as follows, viz: At all elections which shall be held by voters of the said city, for the corporate authorities thereof, the following persons shall be entitled to vote, viz: First, every white male citizen of the State of the age of twenty-one years or upwards, who for at least one year preceding the election, shall have been a house-keeper or the head of a family in said city; second, every person qualified to vote for members of the general assembly of the state, who shall have been a resident of said city for at least one year preceding the election; and third, every white male citizen of the state of the age of twenty-one years or upwards, who at the time of the election shall be the *bona fide* owner of any freehold estate within said city of the value of five hundred dollars: provided always, that no person although in other respects qualified, shall be entitled to vote at any such election, if he shall fail to pay the capitation tax, lawfully assessed or levied upon him for the benefit of said city during the year preceding the election.

2. This act shall be in force from and after its passage.

Section five of an act to incorporate the city of Wheeling in Ohio county, passed March 11, 1836, amended and re-enacted.
Who entitled to vote at city elections for the corporate authorities.
Proviso.
Commencement.

CHAP. 3.—An ACT extending the boundary line of the Corporation of the Town of Buckhannon.

Passed December 19, 1862.

The boundary of the town of Buckhannon in the county of Upshur extended. 1. Be it enacted by the General Assembly, That the boundary of the corporation of the town of Buckhannon in the county of Upshur, be so extended as to include E. J. Colerider within the boundary as follows: beginning on the line of said E. J. Colerider and John L. Smith's land, known in the act passed March 12, 1852, incorporating the said town of Buckhannon, as a tributary of Jawbone run, thence with the said line straight across said Colerider's field to H. F. Westfall's line, thence with said line to the Buckhannon and French creek road, thence with said road to the foot of Trimble's hill to the old corporation line.

Commencement. 2. This act shall be in force from its passage.

CHAP. 4.—An ACT to incorporate the Franklin Insurance Company of Wheeling.

Passed December 19th, 1862.

1. Be it enacted by the General Assembly of Virginia, That *Persons incorporated.* John R. Miller, George Mendel, George K. Wheat, John Zoeckler, Nathaniel C. Arthur, George W. Franzheim, Chester D. Knox, Samuel Harper and James N. Vance, together with such other persons as may hereafter be associated with them, and their successors, the holders of the capital stock hereinafter authorized to be raised, shall be, and they are hereby constituted and made a body politic *Name and style of company.* corporate, under the name and and style of the "Franklin Insurance *With what rights powers and privileges invested.* Company," and by that name and style are invested with all the rights, powers and privileges conferred, and made subject to all the *What rules, regulations and restrictions subjected to.* rules, regulations and restrictions, imposed by the Code of Virginia, applicable to such corporations, and not inconsistent with the provisions of this act.

Capital stock. 2. The capital stock of said company shall not be less than fifty thousand dollars, nor more than five hundred thousand dollars, to *Value of shares.* be divided into shares of the par value of one hundred dollars each.

3. The said company shall have authority and power to make *Subjects of insurance.* insurance against all marine risks, and against any damage or loss by fire, or by any other liability, casualty, or hazard, upon any and *Endowments.* every kind of property, real, personal or mixed, to make insurance *Reversionary payments.* on lives; to grant annuities; to receive endowments; to contract for *May guarantee* reversionary payments; to guarantee the payment of promissory

notes, bills of exchange and other evidences of debt; to lend money on bottomry and respondentia, to cause themselves to be insured against all risks they may have in any property or lives in their own right, or in virtue of any bonds, or advances, or of any policy or contract of insurance.

Payment of promissory notes.
May be insured.

4. The said company shall have power and authority to invest its capital stock, or other funds of the company, in bank or other stocks, in the purchase of bonds issued by this state, the United States, or of any one of the United States, or the bonds of any incorporated company, to lend money upon personal or real security; to discount notes and bills of exchange, and receive the interest in advance, or at the rate of one-half per centum for thirty days; to pay interest upon money deposited with them and give certificates therefor.

May invest its funds in stocks and purchase of bonds of this State, of the United States, or any incorporated company.
May loan money.
May discount notes, or bills of exchange.

5. The secretary of the said company shall be a competent witness, in all suits for or against said company, in all the courts of this commonwealth: provided, he shall not own exceeding twenty-five shares of the capital stock of said company.

Secretary a competent witness.
Proviso.

6. The said capital stock shall be payable by each subscriber, at such time or times as it may be called for by the president and directors of the company, and in such proportions as they may deem necessary; due notice of every such call being given by advertisement published in some newspaper printed in the city of Wheeling; each subscriber, when required so to do by the said president and directors, shall give bond with good and approved personal security in a penalty equal to the par value of the stocks held by such subscriber, payable to said company and conditioned for the prompt payment to said company on every such call thereafter made, until the par value of the stock held by such subscriber shall have been fully paid to said company; and if any subscriber shall fail to pay any call so made by the president and directors upon such share or shares owned or held by him, within twenty days after said call shall have been made under this section, then shall the amount of said call, with interest from the time the same was payable and five per centum damages thereon, be recovered by motion in the name of said company, upon not less then ten days notice, in any court of record in the county or place of residence of the subscriber. Judgment may in like manner be rendered in favor of said company against the obligor, or any, or either of them, of every bond taken under this section upon the like notice of such motion. The said president and directors shall from time to time carefully examine the said bonds, and may at any time require any shareholder to give a new bond with other and approved security in the same pen-

When the capital stock is payable.
Subscribers when required, to give bond.
Condition of bond.
Subscribers failing to pay on any call made by the President and Directors within twenty days after said call, then the amount of said call with interest and five per cent damages may be recovered against him by motion. Upon like notice judgment may be rendered in favor of said company against the obligor or any or either of them on every bond taken under this section. The President and Directors to examine bonds.

alty and with the same condition as such original bond. Every subscriber or shareholder who shall fail to give the bond in this section mentioned, or a new bond in lieu of one originally given, within twenty days after the same shall have been required by the president and directors, the whole balance which may be unpaid upon his stock by every such subscriber or shareholder, with interest thereon, may be recovered by motion as aforesaid; or such shares may, after twenty days notice in some newspaper published in the city of Wheeling, of the time and place of sale, be sold at public auction for ready money and transferred to the purchaser.

Marginal notes: May require new bond. Upon failure of shareholder to give bond, or a new bond in lieu of one originally given, within twenty days after the same shall be required the whole balance unpaid on the stock of such shareholder with interest thereon, may be recovered by motion as aforesaid, or such shares may, after twenty days notice in some newspaper published in the city of Wheeling, may be sold at public auction.

7. The offices of said company shall be managed by a president and nine directors, any five of whom shall constitute a quorum. The directors shall be elected by ballot from amongst the stockholders in general meeting assembled, by a majority of the votes of said stockholders present in person or by proxy, according to a scale of voting to be hereinafter prescribed, and the directors thus chosen shall at their first meeting choose from amongst themselves or the stockholders at large a president and vice-president. The said president, vice-president and directors to continue in office until their successors shall have been duly elected. In case of a vacancy in the offices of president, vice-president or directors, from any cause, the directors may elect others to supply their places for the remainder of the term for which they were chosen.

Marginal notes: Officers of the Company. Number constituting a quorum. How Directors are elected. Terms of office of President, Vice-President & Directors. Vacancy, how filled.

8. The president and directors of said company shall appoint a secretary and such other officers as may be necessary, for the management of their business, and shall allow them suitable compensation for their services.

Marginal note: The President and Directors to appoint Secretary, &c. Compensation.

9. The president and directors shall have power to appoint agents in any part of this state or elsewhere, at their discretion and during their pleasure. They may also take for the security of the company, from their officers or agents, such bond in such penalty and with such condition as they may prescribe.

Marginal note: Agents.

10. The president and directors may adopt such rules, orders, or by-laws not inconsistent with this act or the laws of the land, as they may deem proper and necessary, for regulating and prescribing the duties and powers of the officers and the general management of the company.

Marginal note: President and Directors may adopt rules, orders and by-laws.

11. The scale of voting at all the meetings of the stockholders of the company, shall be one vote for every share of stock not exceeding twenty, one vote for every two shares over twenty, and not exceeding one hundred, and one vote for every four shares exceeding one hundred. Every stockholder not indebted to the company, may at pleasure by power of attorney or in person assign and trans-

Marginal note: Scale of voting.

fer his stock in the company on the books of the same, or any part thereof, not being less than one share, but no stockholder indebted to the company shall be permitted to make a transfer of stock or receive a dividend until such debt is paid, or secured to be paid to the satisfaction of the president and directors.   *Stockholders indebted to company not permitted to make transfer of stock or receive a dividend.*

12. Any three of the persons named in the first section of this act shall be authorised to act as commissioners for receiving subscriptions of stock and organizing the said company. They shall give at least ten day's notice of the time and place when, and the persons under whose superintendence subscriptions of stock will be received; the amount to be paid at the time of subscribing upon each share of stock, and may continue open such books of subscription, from day to day, or from time to time, at their pleasure, until the minimum amount of said stock shall have been subscribed. They shall also appoint the time and place for the first meeting of the shareholders or subscribers. General meetings of the stockholders shall be thereafter held annually or oftener, as the directors may by order or by law, prescribe.   *Who authorized to act as commissioners. Notice.*

13. The stockholders of the company shall not be liable for any loss, damage, or responsibility, other than the property they have in the capital and funds of the company, to the amount of the shares respectively held by them, and any profits arising upon them, not divided.   *To what amount stockholders are responsible.*

14. This company shall be located at the city of Wheeling in the county of Ohio and state of Virginia, at which place their principal office shall be kept.   *Location of Company.*

15. This act shall be in force from its passage, and is hereby made perpetual, reserving to the general assembly of Virginia, the power to alter, amend, or repeal it at pleasure.   *Commencement perpetual. Reservation.*

CHAP. 5.—An ACT to appropriate the residuary fund under the last will and testament of Peter Curran, deceased, to Brooke Academy.

Passed December 20, 1862.

1. Be it enacted by the General Assembly of Virginia, That all the residuary fund of the estate of Peter Curran, late of Brooke county, deceased, under his last will and testament devised to the literary fund of Virginia, is hereby appropriated to Brooke Academy in the county of Brooke, and the executors of said last will and testament, are hereby directed and required to pay to said Brooke   *The residuary fund of the estate of Peter Curran, deceased, appropriated to Brooke Academy. Executors of last will and testament of Peter Curran, deceas-*

ACTS OF THE GENERAL ASSEMBLY.

ed, directed and required to pay all money or other property coming into their possession in the nature of a residuary fund, to Brooke Academy. Academy, all the money or other property which may or shall come to their hands or possession as, or in the nature of a residuary fund of said estate, and which under, and according to the provisions of said will, is payable to the literary fund of Virginia.

Brooke Academy to have all the rights, liberties, and powers relative to said residuary fund that the Literary Fund of Virginia would have had had this Act not been passed. 2. That Brooke Academy shall have all the rights, liberties and powers relative to said residuary fund that the said literary fund of Virginia would have had, had this act not been passed, and to this end may sue for and recover the same, and by all due process of law and chancery, may enforce as discoveries and settlements of executorial accounts deemed necessary.

Authority to sue. Power to sell any real estate owned by it, granted to Brooke Academy. 3. That Brooke Academy shall have and is hereby invested with full power to sell and convey all the real estate, at present owned by it, and any deed for this purpose shall be sufficient, when signed and acknowledged by the president of the board of trustees of said Brooke Academy.

Additional Trustees. 4. That Adam Kuhn and Joseph C. Gist are hereby made and constituted as trustees of said Brooke Academy, in addition to the five trustees thereof, appointed by the act passed on the 6th day of February, 1862.

Commencement. 5. This act shall be in force from its passage.

CHAP. 6.—An ACT to amend and re-enact an Act passed February 8, 1862, entitled an Act staying the collection of certain debts.

Passed December 20, 1862.

The Act passed February 8, '62, entitled an Act staying the collection of certain debts amended and re-enacted. 1. Be it enacted by the General Assembly of Virginia, That the act passed February 8, 1862, entitled an act staying the collection of certain debts, be amended and re-enacted so as to read as follows:

No writs of fieri facias, distress warrant or other process to issue under any judgment or decree heretofore rendered by any Court of this Commonwealth or justice of the peace. 2. Be it enacted by the general assembly of Virginia, That no writ of *fieri facias*, distress warrant, order, or other process, shall issue under any judgment or decree heretofore rendered by any court of record in this commonwealth, or justice of the peace, nor upon any judgment, nor under any decree that may hereafter be rendered by any such court or justice while this act shall remain in force, nor shall there be any sale under any deed of trust, heretofore executed, without the consent of all the parties thereto, nor under any decree or judgment now rendered or that may hereafter be rendered, until otherwise provided by law. And in any case where a levy has been made prior to the passage of this act, the property so levied upon shall be returned to the owner, and the judgment upon which the levy was made shall be a lien upon all the property, both personal and real of the debtor, and shall have

Levy.

Property to be returned to owner, Lien.

ACTS OF THE GENERAL ASSEMBLY. 9

priority over all other judgments against the personal property of such debtor. But an execution shall at the instance of the plaintiff or his agent, be issued, and proceedings had thereunder, as if this act had not been passed, in any case where an affidavit has been filed with the clerk or justice, as the case may be, that the affiant believes that the defendant in such case is removing or intends to remove his effects out of the county where the judgment was rendered.

3. Be it further enacted, That any person may sue for any debt and maintain any action at law or in equity and proceed to judgment therein. And any judgment, execution, order, or decree, now issued or rendered, or that may hereafter be rendered, shall, in addition to the provisions of chapters 186 and 188 of the Code of 1860, constitute a lien on all the estate, both personal and real of the judgment debtor from and after the docketing of any such judgment, as provided for in the third and fourth sections of chapter 186 of the Code of Virginia. This provision shall include all judgments whether rendered by justices of the peace or courts of this commonwealth. A lien on real and personal estate.
What included.

4. Be it further enacted, That nothing herein contained shall be so construed as to interfere with or abridge the laws now in force in relation to attachments and actions of detinue and trover, nor in relation to actions of ejectment and unlawful entry and detainer, nor in relation to the prosecution of criminal offences and the collection of fines, taxes, licenses, county levies and all debts due the commonwealth, but the same may be proceeded in as now provided by law, nor shall this act apply to liabilities on the part of sheriffs, constables or other public officers, either to the state, counties, corporations, or individuals, nor to debts contracted after the 26th day of July, 1861, nor to deeds of trust executed after the 26th day of July, 1861, but payments of and sales under the same, may be enforced and proceeded in as if this act had not been passed, nor shall the time during which this act is in force be computed in any case in which the statute of limitations may come in question. Exceptions.

5. This act shall be in force from its passage, but shall expire on the 1st day of February, 1863. Commencement.
Expiration.

CHAP. 7.—An ACT changing the place of holding an Election in the county of Preston.

Passed December 20, 1862.

1. Be it enacted by the General Assembly of Virginia, That the separate election heretofore authorized to be holden at the Nimes The separate election hereto-

ACTS OF THE GENERAL ASSEMBLY.

fore authorized to be holden at the Nimes House in the 8th magisterial district in Preston county discontinued. The election for said district to be holden at the house of Wm. H. Brown in that district. House in the eighth magisterial district, in Preston county, shall be, and the same is hereby discontinued, and in lieu thereof the election for said election precinct shall be holden at the house of William H. Brown in said district, at which election precinct all persons qualified by law to vote in said district may vote.

Commencement. 2. This act shall be in force from its passage.

CHAP. 8.—An ACT for the relief of Joseph Martiney, late Commissioner of the Revenue for Barbour county.

Passed December 23, 1862.

Auditor directed to issue his warrant in favor of Joseph Martiney for the sum of one hundred and fifty dollars, out of any money in the Treasury not otherwise appropriated. 1. Be it enacted by the General Assembly, That the auditor be, and is hereby directed to issue his warrant in favor of Joseph Martiney for the sum one hundred and fifty dollars, to be paid out of any money in the treasury not otherwise appropriated, being the amount due to said Joseph Martiney from the state for services rendered by him as commissioner of the revenue of Barbour county, for the year 1861.

Commencement. 2. This act shall be in force from its passage.

CHAP. 9.—An ACT for the relief of J. W. Stout, late Commissioner of the Revenue for Pleasants county.

Passed January 9, 1863.

Auditor directed to issue his warrant in favor of J.W. Stout for the sum of one hundred and fifty dollars, to be paid out of any money in the treasury not otherwise appropriated. 1. Be it enacted by the General Assembly, That the auditor be directed to issue his warrant in favor of J. W Stout for the sum of one hundred and fifty dollars, to be paid out of money in the treasury not otherwise appropriated, being the amount due said Stout from the State for service rendered as commissioner of the revenue for the county of Pleasants for the year 1861.

Commencement. 2. This act shall be in force from its passage.

CHAP. 10.—An ACT concerning Stephen W. Downey.

Passed January 9, 1863.

Preamble. WHEREAS, It appears to the General Assembly of Virginia that the county court of Hampshire county, Virginia, has not been organized under the re-organized government of Virginia, and whereas, it appears that Stephen W. Downey, a resident of said county, is desirous of obtaining a certificate in accordance with the provisions of the first section of chapter one hundred and sixty-four of the Code of Virginia, that he has been a resident of said county for one year next preceding, that he is a person of honest demeanor, and is over twenty-one years of age, and that he cannot obtain such certificate by reason of the disorganization of said county.

1. Be it therefore enacted, That it shall be lawful for the county court of any county of this commonwealth, upon satisfactory evidence that the said Stephen W. Downey has resided in the said county of Hampshire for one year next preceding, that he is a person of honest demeanor, and is over twenty-one years of age, to grant him a certificate of the facts, and that such certificate, when so given, shall be as valid as if given in accordance with the provisions of section first of chapter one hundred and sixty-four of the Code of Virginia. *Any Court of this Commonwealth upon satisfactory evidence authorized to grant Stephen W. Downey a certificate of age, residence and character.*

2. This act shall be in force from its passage. *Commencement*

CHAP. 11.—An ACT in relation to Coterminous Coal Lands west of the Blue Ridge Mountains in Virginia.

Passed January 9, 1863.

1. Be it enacted by the General Assembly, That no owner or tenant of any land containing coal west of the Blue Ridge of mountains, shall open or sink, or dig, excavate or work in any coal mine or shaft, on such land within five feet of the line dividing said land from that of another person or persons, without the consent, in writing, of every person interested in or having title to such adjoining lands in possession, reversion, or remainder, or of the guardians of any such persons as may be infants. If any person shall violate this section, he shall forfeit five hundred dollars to any person who may sue for the same. *No owner or tenant of land containing coal west of the Blue Ridge of mountains permitted to open, sink, dig, excavate, or work in any coal mine or shaft, &c.* *Penalty for violation of this section.*

2. The owner, tenant or occupier of any land on which a coal mine is opened and worked, or his agent, shall permit any person interested in or having title to any land coterminous with that in which such coal mine is, to have ingress and egress with surveyors and assistants to explore and survey such mine at his own expense, and not oftener than once a month, for the purpose of ascertaining whether or not the preceding section has been violated. Every owner, tenant, occupant, or agent, who shall refuse such permission, exploration, or survey, shall forfeit twenty dollars for each refusal to the person so refused. *Persons whose land is coterminous, &c.* *But not oftener than once a month.* *Every owner, tenant, occupant or agent refusing &c.*

3. Any justice of the county in which such mine is, before whom

12   ACTS OF THE GENERAL ASSEMBLY.

Who authorized to issue summons and to whom. Upon proof of right of entry, the justice designate an early and convenient time for such entry, &c. complaint of such refusal is made, may issue a summons to such owner, tenant, occupant, or agent, to answer such complaint. On the return of the summons executed, and proof that the complainant has right of entry, and that it has been refused without sufficient cause, the justice shall designate an early and convenient time for such entry to be made, and issue his warrant commanding the sheriff of the county to attend and prevent obstructions and impediments to such entry, exploration and survey. The cost of such *The cost of summons and a fee of three dollars to the Sheriff executing the warrant, &c.* summons, and a fee of three dollars to the sheriff executing the warrant, shall be paid by the person whose refusal caused the complaint. But if the justice dismiss the complaint, the costs shall be paid by the party making it.

Commencement. 4. This act shall be in force from its passage.

CHAP. 12.—An ACT for the relief of Samuel P. Hildreth, Treasurer of the Savings Bank of Wheeling.

Passed January 10, 1863.

Auditor directed to issue his warrant in favor of Samuel P. Hildreth, Treasurer of Savings Bank of Wheeling, for the sum of sixty-two dollars and twenty-seven cts. 1. Be it enacted by the General Assembly of Virginia, That the auditor be, and is hereby directed to issue his warrant in favor of Samuel P. Hildreth, treasurer of the savings bank of Wheeling, for the sum of sixty-two dollars and twenty-seven cents, which sum was by him erroneously paid into the state treasury as a tax on dividends for the year 1861, the bank having been taxed upon its capital for the same year.

Commencement. 2. This act shall be in force from its passage

CHAP. 13.—An ACT authorizing the County Court of Marshall county to re-assess two hundred and six acres of land in Marshall county belonging to Spencer Biddle.

Passed January 12, 1863.

The county court of Marshall county authorized to re-assess two hundred and six acres of land situated in said county belonging to Spencer Biddle. Proviso. 1. Be it enacted by the General Assembly, That the county court of Marshall county be, and is hereby authorized to re-assess two hundred and six acres of land situated in said county, and appearing on the commissioner's books as the property of Spencer Biddle: provided the state shall not be subject to any expenses incurred thereby.

Commencement. 2. This act shall be in force from its passage.

CHAP. 14.—An ACT changing the place of holding an Election in the county of Jackson.

Passed January 13, 1863.

1. Be it enacted by the General Assembly, That the separate election heretofore authorized to be holden at the house of William Slaven in the fifth magisterial district of the county of Jackson, shall be, and the same is hereby discontinued, and in lieu thereof, the usual election for said fifth district, shall be holden at the school house near Noah Staats, in said district, at which election precinct all persons qualified by law to vote in said district may vote. *The separate election heretofore authorized to be holden at the house of Wm Slaven, in the fifth magesterial district of the county of Jackson, discontinued*

2. This act shall be in force from its passage. *Commencement.*

CHAP. 15.—An ACT to authorize Charles H. Kimball, Trustee, to construct and maintain a Tram or Railroad from Franklin Furnace to the Baltimore and Ohio Railroad in the county of Preston.

Passed January 13, 1863.

1. Be it enacted by the General Assembly, That Charles H. Kimball, trustee, be and is hereby authorized to locate and construct a tram road or railroad from the Franklin Furnace in the county of Preston, to a point on the Baltimore and Ohio Railroad at or near the mouth of Raccoon creek in the same county; the land for the said road not to exceed thirty feet in width exclusive of the slopes of cuts and embankments. And for the purpose of enabling the said Charles H. Kimball, trustee, to obtain the title for the land required for the said road and the materials from the land adjacent thereto, proper and necessary for its construction and repair, he, the said Charles H. Kimball, as such trustee, shall be and he is hereby authorized to take the same proceedings as are prescribed in the fifty-sixth chapter of the Code of Virginia in relation to corporations generally. *Charles H. Kimball, Trustee, authrized to locate and construct a tram road or railroad, from Franklin Furnace in Preston county to a point on the Baltimore and Ohio railroad at or near the mouth of Raccoon Creek in the same county. The land for said road not to exceed thirty feet in width exclusive of slopes and embankments. Authorized to proceed as prescribed in 56th Chapter of the Code, to obtain the title to land.*

2. This act may at any time hereafter, be amended or repealed by the general assembly. *May be amended or repealed by General Assembly.*

3. This act shall take effect from and after its passage. *Commencement.*

CHAP. 16.—An ACT providing for the repeal of an Act passed February 13, 1862, entitled "An Act to provide for the extension of time for Sheriffs of the Commonwealth to execute writs of *fieri facias* on certain judgments.

Passed January 14, 1863.

The Act entitled an Act to provide for the extension of time for Sheriffs of this Commonwealth to execute writs of fieri facias on certain judgments, passed February 13, 1862, repealed.

1. Be it enacted by the General Assembly of Virginia, That the act entitled "an act to provide for the extension of time for sheriffs of this commonwealth to execute writs of *fieri facias* on certain judgments, passed February 13, 1862," be and the same is hereby repealed.

Commencement.

2. This act shall be in force from its passage.

CHAP. 17.—An ACT to declare that the Council of the city of Wheeling shall consist of two Boards or Branches.

Passed January 15, 1863.

The Council of the city of Wheeling to consist of two boards

1. Be it enacted by the General Assembly of Virginia, That the council of the city of Wheeling, after the next election of officers for said city, shall consist of two separate and distinct boards, with the

One of the said Boards to be called the first Branch, and the other to be called the second Branch. powers, capacities, and jurisdiction, now by law vested in the council of said city; one of which boards or bodies shall be called the first branch of the council of the city of Wheeling, and the other of which boards shall be called the second branch of the council of said city; and

When consent of both of said Branches required. that no tax shall be levied, no appropriation of money be made, no contract entered into, nor any ordinance, by-law, or order be made

Each Branch to judge of the election and qualification of its own members. or enacted without the consent of both of said branches of said city council. But each branch shall be the judge of the election and

To make all needful rules and regulations for the government of its own body. qualification of its own members, and shall have power to make all needful and proper rules and regulations for the government of its own body, and for the convenient direction and dispatch of its affairs and business.

2. Be it further enacted, That the board created by, and mentioned in the sixth section of the act of the general assembly, entitled "an act to incorporate the city of Wheeling, in Ohio county," passed

Which Board to be called the second Branch. Its capacity power and functions unimpaired. Exception. March 11th, 1836, shall constitute and be called the said second branch of the said city council, and shall be chosen and continue, as is now provided by law, with its existing capacity, power and functions, except in so far as the same are abridged, altered or modified by the provisions of this act.

Of whom the first branch shall consist.

3. The first branch of said council shall consist of two members from each ward of the city, and shall be elected by the persons re-

siding in the respective wards, qualified under existing laws to vote for mayor and members of council. *How elected.*

4. At the first annual election for city officers after the passage of this act, there shall be elected by the qualified voters in each ward, two citizens thereof, to be members of the said first branch of the said city council. The member receiving in each ward the greater number of votes, and otherwise qualified, shall continue in office for two years, and until his successor is qualified; and the other member of each ward, and otherwise qualified, shall continue in office one year, and until his successor is qualified, and thereafter annually there shall be chosen by the qualified voters of each ward, one member of the first branch aforesaid for each ward, who shall continue in office for two years, and until his successor is qualified. *Two citizens of members of the first Branch to be elected at the first annual election after the passage of this act. The member receiving in each ward the greater number of votes to continue in office two years, and until his successor is qualified. The other member of each ward to continue in office one year, and until his successor is qualified.*

5. No person shall be eligible as a member of the first branch, unless he be a citizen of the State, and shall have resided in said city at least three years preceding his election, and is a resident of the ward for which he is chosen. And the first branch, as well as the said other branch, shall have power to fill vacancies occurring in their own body by the appointment of a qualified person; and also to remove a member for misbehavior, provided two-thirds of the whole number of such members shall concur in such removal. *One member of the first Branch to be chosen annually thereafter from each ward. Who eligible as member of the first Branch. Power to fill vacancies. Power of removal Proviso.*

6. At all meetings of the first branch it shall be the duty of the mayor to preside, but in his absence the members present constituting a quorum may appoint from their own body a chairman, pro tempore, and they may adopt such rules and appoint such officers, including a clerk, as they may deem proper for the regulation of their proceedings and the convenient transaction of their business. But the salaries of the officers of each branch shall be ascertained and fixed by the council, as it is by this act created and defined. *Who to preside at meetings of the first Branch. Chairman, pro tempore. Salaries.*

7. It shall require the presence of a majority of the whole number of each branch as fixed by law, to constitute a quorum for the transaction of business, but a smaller number may adjourn from time to time, and compel the attendance of absent members in such way as the council may have provided. *Majority of the whole board necessary to constitute a quorum. A smaller number may adjourn from time to time and compel the attendance of absent members.*

8. The second branch of said council shall appoint one of its own members to preside over its deliberations, who shall be called the president of the second branch of the city council, and it shall be his duty when present, to preside at all meetings thereof, but in his absence, it may appoint one of its own members to preside as president pro tempore. *Who to preside in Second Branch. Duty of presiding officer of Second Branch. President pro tempore.*

9. When the office of mayor of the said city is vacant, the president of the second branch shall be mayor of the city, until such vacancy is filled, except that he shall not preside at the meetings of *When vacancy in office of Mayor to be filled by President of Second Branch. Exception.*

When the Mayor is temporarily absent, who may be permitted to act as Mayor. the first branch; and when the mayor of the city is temporarily absent therefrom, the president of the second branch, may if the council shall so ordain, possess the powers and exercise the duties of mayor during the time the mayor may continue absent from the city.

Propositions involving an appropriation of money, where to originate. 10. All propositions involving an appropriation of money, shall originate in the second branch of said council, but the first branch may propose or concur with amendments, as in other propositions.

Power of Council in reference to this Act. 11. The council of said city, as hereby created, shall have full power to make, pass and execute any ordinance which may be necessary or proper, to carry into effect the true intent and meaning of this act.

Commencement. 12. This act shall be in force from and after its passage.

CHAP. 18.—An ACT to incorporate Logan Tribe No. 21 of the Improved Order of Red Men, in the City of Wheeling.

Passed January 17, 1863.

Names of individuals incorporated. 1. Be it enacted by the General Assembly, That Joseph F. Gachter, Frederick Rolf, William Wegman, Henry Schaffer, and August Hildebright, and such others as are now regularly associated with them, are hereby created a body politic and corporate, under *Made a body politic and corporate.* the name and style of "Logan Tribe No. 21 of the Improved Order *Name and style of incorporation.* of Red Men," in the city of Wheeling and county of Ohio, and by that name shall have perpetual succession and a common seal, may sue and be sued, plead and be impleaded, and may purchase, sell and hold, to them and their successors, for the charitable and benevolent purpose of said Tribe, and no other, not exceeding one full lot of ground in the city of Wheeling, and not exceeding three acres of land within the county of Ohio; and also such personal property and moneys necessary for the purposes aforesaid.

Authorized to make all needful laws and regulations. 2. The said Tribe shall be authorized to make all needful laws and regulations for the management of their property, as a majority of said Tribe may prescribe.

Commencement. May be altered, amended or repealed. 3. This act shall take effect from and after its passage, and may be altered, amended or repealed at the pleasure of the General Assembly.

CHAP. 19.—An ACT to amend the Charter of the Holliday's Cove Railroad Company.

Passed January 19, 1863.

1. Be it enacted by the General Assembly, That the Holliday's Cove Railroad Company, or its lessees, may locate, construct, furnish and work a branch railroad from their terminus on the eastern side of the Ohio river, through the town of Wellsburg, in Brooke county, to the city of Wheeling. *Permission given to.*

2. Be it further enacted, That sections seven, eight, nine, ten, eleven, twelve, and thirteen of "an act to incorporate the Holliday's Cove Railroad Company, passed March 30, 1860," be, and the same are hereby repealed: provided however, that this act shall be of no effect until the Western Transportation company of Pennsylvania named in the eighth section of the act entitled "an act to incorporate the Wheeling Railroad Bridge Company, passed the 3d day of March, 1860," transfer and assign to Thomas Sweeney, and Sobieski Brady, or the survivors of them, any and all right and interest it has in said bridge company, and in the capital stock thereof, and upon such transfer the said Western Transportation Company shall not be liable for any instalments upon said stock accruing thereafter. *Sections repealed.* *Proviso.*

3. This act shall be in force from its passage. *Commencement.*

CHAP. 20.—An ACT changing the place of holding the election in the counties of Hardy and Monongalia.

Passed January 19, 1863.

1. Be it enacted by the General Assembly of Virginia, That the election heretofore authorized by law to be held at Michaels in the sixth magisterial district in Hardy county, be, and the same is hereby abolished, and that in lieu thereof the election hereafter to be held in the sixth district, shall be held at the house now occupied by John W. Athey, in Greenland. *Election heretofore held at Michaels, in Hardy county,abolish'd. To be held at the house now occupied by John W. Athey, in Greenland.*

2. Be it further enacted, that the election precinct held in the county of Monongalia, be discontinued, and that in lieu thereof the regular place of voting for said precinct shall hereafter be held at the house of James Arnett in the town of Arnettsville. *Election precinct in Monongalia county, discontinued. The election to be held at the house of James Arnett, of Arnettsville.*

3. This act shall be in force from its passage. *Commencement.*

CHAP. 21.—An ACT establishing a place of voting at Rockford School-house, in the third Magisterial District of Harrison County.

Passed January 19, 1863.

An election precinct established at Rockford School House in Harrison county.

1. Be it enacted by the General Assembly of Virginia, That an election precinct be, and the same is hereby established at Rockford school-house, in the third magisterial district of Harrison county, and that said school-house shall hereafter be a regular place of voting in said county in all elections required by law to be held in the counties of this commonwealth.

Commencement.

2. This act shall be in force from its passage.

CHAP. 22.—An ACT to authorize Charles B. Waggener, trustee, to sell certain property in Mason county.

Passed January 19, 1863.

Preamble.

WHEREAS, it is represented to the General Assembly, That one William B. Robbins executed three several trust deeds, granting certain lands in Mason county to Abner W. Hogg to secure the payment of several bonds, in said deeds described, to John McCullock, Moses Michael and John Hall, which deeds bear date respectively on the fifth day of August, one thousand eight hundred and fifty-three, the twenty-third day of May, one thousand eight hundred and fifty-three, and the twenty-fourth day of May, one thousand eight hundred and fifty-three, which bonds, although due and payable, remain unsatisfied; that the said Abner W. Hogg having become insane, Charles B. Waggener, by a decree of the circuit court of said county, at the spring term of the year one thousand eight hunred and sixty-one was appointed to act as trustee instead of the said Abner W. Hogg, and that he, the said Charles B. Waggener, by advertisement, as provided for in said deeds, gave public notice that he would sell the said property on the fourth Saturday of January, ene thousand eight hundred and sixty-three; that the said William B. Robbins is not an inhabitant of this state, and that the said property, consisting of mineral lands, with salt furnaces and coal-works erected thereon, is now in a state of decay and dilapidation, and rapidly depreciating in value; and that a sale of the same at an early day will be beneficial to both the debtor and creditors; therefore,

Charles B. Waggener authorized to sell certain property.

1. Be it enacted by the General Assembly of Virginia, That it shall be lawful for the said Charles B. Waggener to sell the said

ACTS OF THE GENERAL ASSEMBLY. 19

property on the said fourth Saturday of January, one thousand eight hundred sixty-three, or on any subsequent day to which he may continue or postpone the said sale, anything in the act of February the eighth, one thousand eight hundred and sixty-two, entitled "an act to amend and re-enact the act passed July the twenty-sixth, one thousand eight hundred and sixty-one, entitled 'an act staying the collection of certain debts,'" or in the act passed December the twenty-second, one thousand eight hundred and sixty-two, to amend and re-enact the said act of February the eighth, one thousand eight hundred and sixty-two, to the contrary notwithstanding.

2. This act shall be in force from its passage. Commencement.

CHAP. 23. —An ACT to amend the Charter of the Wheeling Railroad Bridge Company.

Passed January 19, 1863.

Be it enacted by the General Assembly, That the first section of "an act to incorporate the Wheeling Railroad Bridge Company," passed March 30, 1860, be amended and re-enacted so as to read as follows: The first section of an Act to incorporate the Wheeling Railroad Bridge Co.

1. Be it enacted by the General Assembly, That it shall be lawful for Thomas Sweeney, Jno. C. Campbell, Sobieski Brady, Chester D. Hubbard and Zachariah Jacob, or any three of them, to open books of subscription in the city of Wheeling, and at such other place or places as they may direct upon ten days notice, and under the direction of such agent or agents as they or a majority of them may appoint, for the purpose of receiving subscriptions of stock, in shares of one hundred dollars each, to an amount not less than two thousand and not more than ten thousand shares, to constitute a joint stock company to be called "The Wheeling Railroad Bridge Company," by which name the said company shall have authority to erect and maintain a railroad bridge across the Ohio river at any point it may select not farther south than the mouth of McMahon's creek, and not farther north than the northern end of Zane's Island, opposite the city of Wheeling: provided that the said bridge shall be so constructed as to leave an unobstructed headway over the channel of said river of not less than ninety feet above low water mark, and an unobstructed water-way between the piers of said bridge next the channel of not less than three hundred feet, and to connect within the corporate limits of Wheeling, their said bridge

by railway with such railways as may terminate at or near Wheeling, as is hereinafter provided.

Fourth section of said Act amended and re-enacted.
2. The fourth section of said act shall read as follows:

Lawful for company to establish rates of toll.
"§4. It shall be lawful for said company to establish rates of toll, which it may charge and collect on all locomotives, tenders, express, baggage and burden cars which may pass over said bridge and connections, and for such freight, passengers or other things as may be transported over said bridge and connections: provided, that the rates of toll shall be uniform and without discrimination as to all railroad companies, or persons and companies running or working a railroad or railroads which have their terminus on either side of the Ohio river at or near the city of Wheeing.

Proviso.

"And it is expressly enacted that all freight and passengers passing over or to pass over said bridge eastward or westward, shall where a transfer or change of cars is had or may be necessary from one car to another, within twenty-five miles of said city on either side of the Ohio river, be transferred and make such change of cars east of the Ohio river and not south of a point opposite to the mouth of McMahon's creek, and that the passenger trains on the Baltimore and Ohio Railroad Company's railroad and those of the Central Ohio Railroad shall commence and terminate their trips, at and from the city of Wheeling, giving to the passengers holding through tickets the privilege of going from such point of transfer, to and from the city of Wheeling, without additional charge, notice of which shall be posted in the cars of said companies respectively."

Transfer of passengers.

B. & O. Railroad and C. O. Railroad companies to commence and terminate their trips at the city of Wheeling.

The fourteenth section of said act repealed.
3. The fourteenth section of said act is hereby repealed.

The fifteenth section of said act amended and re-enacted.
4. The fifteenth section of said act shall read as follows:
"§15. The said company shall be subject to the provisions of the thirty-fifth section of the act entitled 'an act prescribing certain general regulations for the incorporation of railroad companies,' passed March eleventh, eighteen hundred and thirty-seven."

The sixteenth section of said act repealed.
5. The sixteenth section of said act is hereby repealed.

Commencement.
6. This act shall be in force from its passage.

CHAP. 24.—An ACT declaring a part of Elk River a lawful fence.

Passed January 20, 1863.

Part of Elk River declared a lawful fence.
1. Be it enacted by the General Assembly of Virginia, That so much of Elk river as lies between the mouth of Sand creek and the lower line of the land of John D. Young on the northwest side thereof, in the county of Kanawha, be, and the same is hereby declared a lawful fence.

Commencement.
2. This Act shall be in force from its passage.

CHAP. 25.—An ACT authorizing the County Court of Preston County to re-assess one hundred and ninety and one-fourth acres of land in Preston county belonging to Caleb Conn.

Passed January 20, 1863.

1. Be it enacted by the General Assembly of Virginia, That the county Court of Preston county be, and the same is hereby authorized to re-assess one hundred and ninety and one-fourth acres of land situated on Tunnel Hill, in the county of Preston, and appearing on the commissioner's books of said county as the property of Caleb Conn: provided, the state shall not be subject to any expenses incurred thereby. *County Court of Preston county authorized to re-assess land in said county belonging to Caleb Conn. Proviso.*

2. This act shall be in force from its passage. *Commencement.*

CHAP. 26.—An ACT to incorporate the Pittsburg and Steubenville Coal Company.

Passed January 20, 1863.

1. Be it enacted by the General Assembly of Virginia, That James Andrews, Robert Henderson, John Scott, Thomas A. Scott, and Thomas L. Jewett, and such other persons as may hereafter be associated with them, shall be, and are hereby incorporated and made a body politic and corporate, by the name of "the Pittsburg and Steubenville Coal Company," for the purpose of mining coal, and transporting coal to market, and they are hereby invested with the rights, powers and privileges, and made subject to all the rules, regulations and restrictions provided and prescribed in the Code of Virginia, and any laws amendatory thereof, so far as the same are applicable and not inconsistent with the powers and rights herein granted. *Incorporation. Style of company. Made subject to the rules, regulations and restrictious of the Code of Virginia.*

2. The capital stock of said company shall not be less than twenty-five, nor more than two hundred thousand dollars, to be divided into shares of one hundred dollars each, and the said James Andrews, Robert Henderson, John Scott, Thomas A. Scott, and Thomas L. Jewett, or any three of them, may open books of subscription to the capital stock at such time and place as they may deem expedient; and they may receive subscriptions in land and personal property at such a rate as may be agreed upon, and fix the amount to be paid by each subscriber at the time of making his subscription. In all general meetings of the stockholders of said company, each stockholder shall have as many votes as he has shares. *Shares. Subscriptions. Proportion of votes.*

3. The stockholders may elect not less than five, nor more than nine directors, who of their own number, may elect a president. The president and directors shall have power to make by-laws for the management of the company; to alter and amend the same; appoint agents and clerks and discharge the same at pleasure; to borrow money, not exceeding at any one time, the amount of its capital stock paid in, and may secure the payment of such debt by mortgage of the real or personal property of the company.

Directors. Power of President and Directors.

4. It shall be lawful for said company to construct a railroad not exceeding two miles in length, for the purposes of the company, from some point near the Ohio river on the Holliday's Cove railroad, to a point on the Ohio river, suitable for shipping purposes, and to construct wharves, turn-outs, protections from ice, and whatever may be necessary for the purposes of the company. They may acquire lands, not exceeding in quantity fifty acres, and purchase the coal privilege of lands; and they shall have power to build their road and improvements upon the lands of persons, other than those of said company, with the consent of the owner of such lands, or by contract with such owner. And the said company may navigate, by steamers and barges, the Ohio and Mississippi rivers and their tributaries, in carrying their coal to market.

Authorized to construct a railroad.

May acquire not exceeding fifty acres of land.

5. The stock of the company shall be transferable under such regulations and restrictions as the president and directors may establish from time to time.

6. This act shall be in force from its passage.

Commencement.

CHAP. 27.—An ACT to amend and re-enct the tenth section of chapter 170 of the Code of Virginia.

Passed January 22, 1863.

1. Be it enacted by the General Assembly of Virginia, That the tenth section of chapter one hundred and seventy of the Code of Virginia, edition of 1860, be amended and re-enacted so as to read as follows, viz:

Section ten of chapter 170 of the Code of 1860 amended and re-enacted.

"§10. On affidavit that a defendant is not a resident of this state, or that diligence has been used by or on behalf of the plaintiff to ascertain in what county or corporation he is, without effect, or that process, directed to the officer of the county or corporation in which he resides, or is, or has been twice delivered to such officer more than ten days before the return day, and being returned without being executed, or that the defendant in any suit has left the county or corporation wherein the cause of action or any part thereof arose, and wherein said suit is or may be pending, and that process directed to the officer of the county where such defendant resides, or is, cannot be delivered to such officer or executed by him, by reason of insurrection, rebellion or armed resistance to the enforcement of the laws, an order of publication may be entered against such defendant; and in any suit in equity where the bill states that the names of any persons interested in the subject to be divided or disposed of, are unknown, and makes such persons defendants, by the general description of parties unknown, on affidavit of the fact, that the said names are unknown, an order of publication may be entered against such unknown parties; any order under this section may be entered either in court or at the rules: In a proceeding by petition there may be an order of publication in like manner as in a suit in equity.

2. This act shall take effect from and after its passage. Commencement.

CHAP. 28.—An ACT to amend and re-enact the first and seventh sections of chapter forty-six of the Code of Virginia.

Passed January 22, 1863.

1. Be it enacted by the General Assembly, That the first section of chapter forty-six of the Code of Virginia, (edition of 1860), be amended and re-enacted so as to read as follows: *Section one of chapter forty six of the Code of 1860 amended and re-enacted.*

"§1. When the auditor of public Accounts shall disallow, either in whole or part, any such claim against the commonwealth as is provided for by the twelfth section of the forty-sixth chapter, the person prosecuting such claim may petition the circuit court for the county in which the seat of government is for redress; and when a person has any other claim against the commanwealth, redress may be obtained in the said court by a petition or by a bill in chancery, according to the nature of the case."

2. Be it further enacted, That the seventh section of chapter forty-six be amended and re-enacted so as to read as follows: *Section seven of chapter forty six amended and re-enacted.*

"§7. There shall be brought and prosecuted in the circuit court of the county in which the seat of government is, all suits in which it may be necessary or proper to make any of the following public persons a party defendant as representing the commonwealth, to-wit: the governor, attorney-general, treasurer, or auditor of public accounts, or in which it may be necessary or proper to make any of the following public corporations, parties defendants, to-wit: the board of the literary fund, board of public works, or any other pub-

ACTS OF THE GENERAL ASSEMBLY.

lic corporation composed of officers of the governmen, of the funds and property of which the commonwealth is sole owner, or in which it shall be attepted to injoin or otherwise suspend or effect any judgment or decree on behalf of the commonwealth obtained in any circuit court holden in she county of Ohio or the city of Richmond, or any execution issued on such judgment or decree."

Commencement. 3. This act shall be in force from its passage.

CHAP. 29.—An ACT authorizing Messrs. Smith & Williams to sell goods in Jackson county.

Passed January 24, 1863.

Sheriff authorized to issue a license to.
1. Be it enacted by the General Assembly of Virginia, That the sheriff of Jackson county be, and is hereby authorized to issue a merchant's license for the year 1862, to Messrs. Smith & Williams in the said county of Jackson, without requiring the payment of the tax lawfully imposed thereon, provided that the said sheriff of Jackson county shall require the said Smith & Williams to surrender the license now in their possession authorizing them to sell goods in Roane county.

Proviso.

Commencement. 2. This act shall be in force from its passage.

CHAP. 30.—An ACT providing for the return of the Special Election for a Representative in the seventh Congressional district, held on the 15th day of January, 1863.

Passed January 24, 1863.

The Clerk of the County Court authorized to make returns.
1. Be it enacted by the General Assembly, That the clerk of the county court authorized by law to make returns of the election held on the 15th day of January, 1863, for a representative in congress for the seventh district, be and is hereby authorized and required to ascertain the result and grant certificates thereof, at any time within the thirty days allowed therefor.

Commencement. 2. This act shall be in force from its passage.

CHAP. 31.—An ACT to incorporate the Clarksburg Coal and Iron Company.

Passed January 24, 1863.

1. Be it enacted by the General Assembly of the State of Virginia, That John Robinson, M. P. O'Hern, and James W. Stoddard,

and such other persons as may hereafter be associated with them, shall be, and they are hereby incorporated and made a body politic and corporate for the purpose of mining coal and iron ore and manufacturing iron and other articles, and vending the same under the name and style of the "Clarksburg Coal and Iron Company," and are hereby invested with all the rights, powers and privileges conferred on such bodies politic and to continue for fifty years. *Incorporated. Name and style of Company.*

2. That the capital stock of said company shall be two hundred and fifty thousand dollars, divided in shares of twenty dollars each, that the subscription may be made in money, real and personal estate; the real and personal estate may be taken at the rate agreed upon by the contracting parties; and the president and directors, or a majority of them, shall have full power to manage the affairs of the company. *Capital stock. Shares. Subscriptions.*

3. The president and directors shall have power to purchase and hold any other mining property and land, not to exceed five thousand acres, in any county in the State of Virginia. *President and directors may purchase land not to exceed five thousand acres.*

4. The president and directors, or a majority of them, shall have power to issue coupon or other bonds, but not to exceed one-half of the capital stock of said company, and the property of the company shall be security therefor. *Power to issue coupon or other bonds.*

5. This act shall take effect from its passage. *Commencement.*

CHAP. 32.—An ACT appropriating forty thousand dollars to the Lunatic Asylum west of the Allegheny Mountains.

Passed January 27, 1863.

1. Be it enacted by the General Assembly, That the sum of forty thousand dollars be, and is hereby appropriated out of any moneys in the treasury, not otherwise appropriated, to the Lunatic Asylum west of the Allegheny mountains, to be expended under the direction of the board of Directors, first for the finishing and furnishing of the south wing of said Asylum ready for use, and the residue of said appropriation shall be for the further prosecution and erection of the main building connected with said south wing, and the money to be drawn from time to time from the treasury as the work may progress. *Forty thousand dollars appropriated to the Lunatic Asylum. How to be expended.*

2. This act shall be in force from its passage. *Commencement.*

CHAP. 33.—An ACT providing for the removal of criminals and criminal causes from the counties of Braxton and Randolph to the county of Lewis.

Passed January 28, 1863.

Lawful for the county or circuit courts of Braxton & Randolph counties to make an order for the transfer to the county or circuit court of Lewis of any criminal cause now pending therein.

1. Be it enacted by the General Assembly of Virginia, That it will be lawful for the county or circuit court of the counties of Braxton and Randolph to make an order for the removal and transfer to the county or circuit court of Lewis county for trial therein, any criminal cause now pending therein, or which may hereafter be commenced in the courts of the said counties. And the said courts of the said county of Lewis have and exercise the same jurisdiction over the same as if the said cause had commenced in the courts of the said county of Lewis. And if there be no courts organized in said counties of Braxton and Randolph, it will be lawful for the justices of said counties to commit any criminal into the custody of the jailor of Lewis county, and he shall receive into his custody any such criminal so committed to him or his deputy, and keep as if such criminal had been committed by a justice of the peace for the county of Lewis.

Commencement. 2. This act shall be in force from its passage.

CHAP. 34.—An ACT authorizing the Board of Public Works to hire out certain convicts.

Passed January 28, 1863.

Preamble. Whereas, it is represented to the General Assembly of Virginia, That there are convicts who have been sentenced to the penitentiary, since the existence of hostilities and the re-organization of the state government; and whereas, there being no penitentiary in the loyal portion of the state, and whereas by an act of the general assembly, passed on the 26th of July, 1861, the governor was authorized to use the jails of the several counties of this commonwealth for the confinement of said convicts.

The Board of Public Works authorized to hire out certain convicts.

1. Be it therefore enacted by the General Assembly of Virginia, That the board of public works, be, and they are hereby authorized to hire out said convicts so confined in the several county jails, to a superintendent or superintendents of works of internal improvements, undertaken by the State, in whole or in part, or any other

works of a corporation or individual, and the wages for the labor of such convicts, requiring of such superintendents such assurance for the safe keeping, together with all the necessary provisions to carry out this act, either by appointing a suitable overseer over such convicts, or otherwise.

2. This act shall be in force from its passage. *Commencement.*

CHAP. 35.—An ACT to repeal and re-enact section second of an Act to authorize the Trustees of Brooke Academy to transfer their property to the Meade Collegiate Institute, and to authorize said Institute to transfer the same property to the Trustees hereinafter appointed, passed February 6, 1862, to read as follows:

Passed January 28, 1863.

1. Be it enacted by the General Assembly of Virginia, That the second section of an act to authorize the trustees of Brooke Academy to transfer their property to the Meade Collegiate Institute, and to authorize said Institute to transfer the same property to the trustees hereinafter appointed, passed February 6, 1862, be amended and re-enacted so as to read as follows: *Section second amended and re-enacted.*

"§2. Be it enacted, that Hugh W. Crothers, Danforth Brown, David Fleming, Obadiah Langfitt, Samuel George, Adam Kuhn, Joseph C. Gist, William H. Harvey, Joseph Applegate, John D. Wier, and Thomas Everett, be, and they are hereby appointed and made trustees of the Brooke Academy, a majority of whom shall have power to act and to fill all vacancies occurring in their own body. And the said trustees are hereby authorized to take possession of all real estate formerly belonging to said Brooke Academy, whenever the same shall have been conveyed to them as hereinafter provided for, and to collect and receive all moneys due or in any wise belonging to or held in the name of Brooke Academy, and apply the same to the best advantage for an academy of education within the intent and meaning of its former charter. And they are hereby authorized to purchase other real estate for the purpose of enlarging said academy and of adding thereto a female seminary, whether such real estate adjoins the aforesaid real estate or not, and to this end may accept donations in land, money or other property."

2. This act shall be in force from and after its passage. *Commencement.*

CHAP. 36.—An ACT providing for the amendment and re-enactment of the eleventh section of chapter twenty-ninth of the Code of eighteen hundred and sixty.

Passed January 29, 1863.

Section eleven of chapter 29 of the Code of 1860 amended and re-enacted

1. Be it enacted by the General Assembly of Virginia, That the eleventh section of chapter twenty-ninth of the Code of eighteen hundred and sixty, be amended and re-enacted so as to read as follows:

"§11. No proceeding shall be had in any court at law or in equity, or on any execution against the person or property of one who has volunteered, or who has been drafted and ordered into actual service, (whether of the state or of the United States), or against his surety from the time such person shall be ordered to the place of rendezvous until three months after his term of service shall have expired. In any case where a suit or other proceeding has been commenced before the passage of this act, against any such person or his sureties, it shall not be necessary for him or his sureties to set forth the fact that any such person against whom any suit or other proceeding may have been commenced, has volunteered or been drafted and ordered into actual service by a formal plea in abatement or other plea, but an affidavit in writing of any such person, or agent, that such person has volunteered or been drafted into the actual service, and as satisfactory proof thereof, the court or justice before whom such proceedings may be pending shall order such suit or proceedings to be stayed until the expiration of three months after the term of service of any such person shall have expired, when the same may be proceeded in as if this act had not been passed. This act shall not apply to any person who shall have received the money of another in a fiduciary character, nor as an officer of this commonwenlth, or of any court, nor to any of his sureties, nor to any person who shall have employed a substitute to perform his term of duty, nor shall it prevent the granting or reinstating of any injunction.

Commencement. 2. This act shall be in force from its passage.

CHAP. 37.—An ACT declaring the North Fork of Fishing Creek, in the county of Wetzel, a public highway.

Passed January 29, 1863.

A portion of the North Fork

1. Be it enacted by the General Assembly of Virginia, That the north fork of Fishing creek, in the county of Wetzel, from the

main fork up to Jeremiah H. King's mills, be, and the same is hereby declared a public highway for the transportation of boats, lumber, &c.   *Fishing Creek declared a public highway.*

2. Be it further enacted, that it shall be unlawful to obstruct said navigation by the erection of mill-dams, or otherwise.   *Unlawful to obstruct navigation*

3. This act shall be in force from its passage.   *Commencement.*

CHAP. 38.—An ACT providing for the removal of Criminal Causes from the County of Tucker to the County of Preston.

Passed January 29, 1863.

1. Be it enacted by the General Assembly of Virginia, That it will be lawful for the county or circuit courts of Tucker county to make an order for the transfer and removal to the county or circuit court of Preston county for trial therein, any criminal cause now pending therein, or which may hereafter be commenced in the said county, and the courts of Preston county shall have and exercise the same jurisdiction over and for the trial of any such person so removed, as if the same had been commenced in the courts of the said Preston county.   *Courts of Tucker county to transfer criminal causes to Preston county.*

2. This act shall be in force from its passage.   *Commencement.*

CHAP. 39.—An ACT allowing mileage to the Delegates of the Convention.

Passed January 30, 1863.

1. Be it enacted by the General Assembly, That the delegates to the convention which is to assemble at the city of Wheeling on the twelfth day of February, 1863, shall be entitled to the same mileage as is now allowed by law to members of the general assembly.   *Delegates to Convention entitled to mileage*

2. This act shall be in force from its passage.   *Commencement.*

CHAP. 40.—An ACT to amend and re-enact the Act passed May the 15th, 1862, entitled "An Act to re-organize the Kanawha Board.

Passed January 30, 1863.

1. Be it enacted by the General Assembly, That sections four and five of the act passed May the 15th, 1862, be amended and re-enacted so as to read as follows:

ACTS OF THE GENERAL ASSEMBLY.

Section four amended and re-enacted.

"§4. The board of public works, when in their opinion the services of such an officer are required, shall appoint a general superintendent, who shall have supervision of both the Kanawha river and road, whose duty it shall be to collect from the gate-keepers, quarterly, the net proceeds of the tolls collected by said gate-keepers, and keep such road in repair by the use of said tolls and pay over the residue to the Kanawha board for the river improvement; also, to take charge of and secure for the use of the board, all the boats, tools and other property now on the river, which was procured by the Kanawha board in and for the improvement of the Kanawha river and road, and manage and superintend the improvement of the river subject to the control of said Kanawha board, and shall make quarterly returns to said board, of his collections and disbursements, and shall receive for his services annually, a sum not exceeding one thousand dollars."

Section five amended and re-enacted.

"§5. The said Kanawha board shall annually make full report to the board of public works, of all their acts and doings, pertaining to said river and road improvement."

Commencement. 2. This act shall be in force from its passage.

CHAP. 41.—An ACT to legalize the appointment of Ferdinand Lewis, as Administrator of the estate of Solomon Michael, Sr., late of Hardy county.

Passed January 30, 1863.

Appointment of Ferdinand Lewis confirmed.

1. Be it enacted by the General Assembly of Virginia, That the appointment made by Abijah Dolly, a justice of the peace in and for the county of Hardy, in the state of Virginia, of Ferdinand Lewis as the administrator of the personal estate of Solomon Michael, sr., deceased, late of Hardy county, be, and the same is hereby declared legal and binding in law. And that all the acts and proceedings of said administrator have the same force and effect as though said appointment and qualification had been made and done by the county court of said county of Hardy.

2. In the event of there being no court or clerk in the county of Hardy, the bond executed by Ferdinand Lewis, with William Michael and John Michael, as his securities in said administration,

Bond authorized to be filed in Preston County Court.

shall be filed and there preserved in the clerk's office of the county court of Preston county, and shall be in all respects as binding as though given before the county court of Hardy county, and filed in the clerks office of said court of Hardy county.

Commencement. 3. This act shall be in force from its passage.

ACTS OF THE GENERAL ASSEMBLY.   21

CHAP. 42.—An ACT for the relief of E. H. Mayo.

Passed January 30, 1863.

1. Be it enacted by the General Assembly, That E. H. Mayo, of Kanawha county, be, and is hereby released from the payment of a merchant's license imposed upon him for the year 1862.

2. This act shall be in force from its passage.

E. H. Mayo released from the payment of a merchant's license.

Commencement.

CHAP. 43.—An ACT authorizing the Governor to postpone the May Elections for the year 1863.

Passed January 30, 1863.

1. Be it enacted by the General Assembly, That if the convention and people of the proposed state of West Virginia shall ratify the change in their constitution proposed by congress, then the governor of this commonwealth shall issue his proclamation, suspending and postponing, until the fourth Thursday of October, within the boundaries of the said proposed state, the elections appointed by law to be held on the fourth Thursday of May next; and if the said proposed state, shall within the said period, become one of the United States, such suspension and postponement shall become perpetual.

2. This act shall be in force from its passage.

Elections on the fourth Thursday of May, postponed.

Commencement.

CHAP. 44.—An ACT for the relief of George Fisher, Commissioner of the Revenue for Lewis county.

Passed January 30, 1863.

1. Be it enacted by the General Assembly, That the auditor be, and is hereby directed to issue his warrant in favor of George Fisher, for the sum of seventy-five dollars, to be paid out of any money in the treasury not otherwise appropriated, being the amount due said George Fisher for services rendered by him as commissioner of the revenue for Lewis county for the year 1861.

2. This act shall be in force from its passage.

Auditor to pay George Fisher, seventy-five dollars.

Commencement.

CHAP. 45.—An ACT to amend the second section of chapter four of the Code of Virginia in relation to districting the State for Representatives in Congress.

Passed January 30, 1863.

Section second amended and re-enacted.

1. Be it enacted by the General Assembly, That the second section of chapter four of the Code of Virginia, be, and the same is hereby amended and re-enacted so as to read as follows:

Apportionment of representatives.
No. of districts.

"§2. The number of members to which this state is entitled in the house of representatives of the United States, shall continue apportioned amongst the several counties, cities, towns and corporations of the state arranged into eleven districts, numbered as follows, that is to say:

First district.

"The counties of Accomac, Northampton, Northumberland, Westmoreland, Richmond, Essex, Lancaster, Middlesex, King and Queen, King William, New Kent, Gloucester, Matthews, York, James City, Elizabeth City, Warwick, Charles City, King George, and Caroline, with a population of 129,201, form the first congressional district.

Second district.

"And the counties of Princess Anne, Norfolk and City, Nansemond, Isle of Wight, Southampton, Sussex, Surry, Prince George, Dinwiddie, Greenville, and Brunswick, with a population of 129,901, form the second congressional district.

Third district.

"And the counties of Stafford, Spottsylvania, Orange, Culpeper, Rappahannock, Louisa, Hanover, Henrico, Richmond City, and Goochland, with a population of 133,139, form the third congressional district.

Fourth district.

"And the counties of Mecklenburg, Lunenburg, Charlotte, Appomattox, Prince Edward, Nottoway, Buckingham, Cumberland, Amelia, Powhattan, Chesterfield, Fluvanna, Amherst, and Nelson, with a population of 135,829, form the fourth congressional district.

Fifth district.

"And the counties of Patrick, Henry, Franklin, Pittsylvania, Halifax, Campbell, Bedford, and Roanoke, with a population of 132,680, form the fifth congressional district.

Sixth district.

"And the counties of Rockingham, Augusta, Rockbridge, Highland, Bath, Allegheny, Bottetourt, Albemarle, Page, Greene, Madison, and Craig, with a population of 131,380, form the sixth congressional district.

Seventh district.

"And the counties of Alexandria, Berkeley, Frederick, Shenandoah, Jefferson, Clark, Warren, Loudoun, Fauquier, Fairfax, and Prince William, with a population of 133,082, form the seventh congressional district.

Eighth district.

"And the counties of Lee, Scott, Wise, Buckhannon, Russell,

Washington, Grayson, Smythe, Tazewell, Bland, Wythe, Carroll, Pulaski, Giles, Montgomery, and Floyd, with a population of 129,-934, form the eighth congressional district.

"And the counties of Ohio, Hancock, Brooke, Marshall, Wetzel, Tyler, Pleasants, Doddridge, Harrison, Ritchie, Wood, Wirt, Gilmer, Calhoun, and Roane, with a population of 114,141, form the ninth congressional district. *Ninth district.*

"And the counties of Kanawha, Jackson, Mason, Putnam, Cabell, Clay, Wayne, Logan, Boone, Braxton, Nicholas, McDowell, Wyoming, Raleigh, Fayette, Mercer, Monroe, and Greenbrier, with a population of 117,378, form the tenth congressional district. *Tenth district.*

"And the counties of Taylor, Marion, Monongalia, Preston, Tucker, Lewis, Barbour, Upshur, Webster, Pocahontas, Randolph, Pendleton, Hardy, Hampshire, and Morgan, with a population of 114,807, form the eleventh congressional district." *Eleventh district*

2. This act shall be in force from its passage. *Commencement.*

CHAP. 46.—An ACT to incorporate the Citizens' Railway Company of the City of Wheeling.

Passed January 30, 1863.

1. Be it enacted by the General Assembly, That John L. Hobbs, S. H. Woodward, Chester D. Hubbard, Joshua Bodley, John List, Robert Crangle, Andrew J. Sweeney, Robert Irwin, or a majority of them be, and they are hereby appointed commissioners to open books for the purpose of receiving subscriptions to the capital stock of the company hereby incorporated, by the name, style and title of the "Citizens' Railway Company," with power to lay out and construct a railway of single track, and the necessary sidlings and switches, which may commence at any point not farther south than the southern line of Ohio county, and may run through the town of South Wheeling of Fifth street to Denny street, along Denny street to Jacob street, along Jacob street into the city of Wheeling by said street to Chapline street, along Chapline street to First street, along First street to Main street, along Main street to John street, along John street to Market street, along Market street to Madison street, along Madison street to Main street, along Main street to the Martin's Ferry Landing, and from Main street along Madison street across the suspension bridge and along Zane street, and across the the western bridge to the limits of the state of Virginia. The consent of the several corporations through whose streets the *Incorporators. Name of Company. Powers. Consent.*

3

said railway passes having been first obtained for the use of said streets, and the said company are hereby empowered and authorized to use any other streets of said corporations for their business, when a like consent is obtained.

Capital stock.

Shares

2. That the capital stock of the said company shall consist of not less than twenty-five thousand nor more than one hundred thousand dollars, which shall be divided into shares of fifty dollars each.

3. That as soon as twenty-five thousand dollars of said stock is subscribed for *bona fide,* the said commissioners, or a majority of them, may call a meeting of the said subscribers—giving at least ten days notice of the time and place thereof, by publication in one or more newspapers published in the city of Wheeling, and if a majority of said stockholders is not represented on that day in person or by proxy, the meeting shall stand adjourned from day to day until a majority of said stock shall be represented. The stockholders at said meeting shall proceed to organize said corporation, and shall choose by a majority of the votes represented at said meeting by ballot, five directors, all of whom shall be citizens of Ohio county, who shall choose one of their number to be president, all of whom shall serve until the time fixed in the by-laws for the next annual meeting of the stockholders, or until their successors are regularly and lawfully chosen, that each and every member of said corporation shall be entitled to vote for each share of stock held by him or her; and that the directors of said company may at any time increase the capital stock to the maximum limit of $100,000, and the Weeeling and Belmont Bridge Company are hereby authorized and empowered to subscribe to said stock to an amount not exceeding $10,000.

Notice of meeting.

Organization.

Terms.

May increase the capital stock. Wheeling and Belmont Bridge Company may subscribe.

4. That as soon as the stockholders shall have elected the directors as aforesaid, the said stockholders shall become a body corporate in deed and in law by the name, style and title of "The Citizens' Railway Company," and by said name they shall have perpetual succession with power to make a corporate seal, and the same to alter, modify and renew at pleasure, and to ordain, establish and put in execution such by-laws, ordinances, rules and regulations, as shall appear necessary and convenient for the said corporation and not being contrary to the Constitution of the United States, nor of this commonwealth, and shall be capable of taking and holding their capital stock and the increase of profits, and of purchasing, taking receiving and holding all such real estate and personal property as may be necessary and convenient to enable them to carry on the business and traffic of their said road with economy facility and dispatch, and the same to exchange, barter, sell, let or lease on ground rent, mortgage or lease, or otherwise dispose of at their

pleasure, and of suing and being sued, pleading and being impleaded by the corporate name, and shall have generally all the rights, privileges, franchises and incidents belonging and appertaining to a corporation, and the right of doing all and every other matter and thing which a corporation may lawfully do.

5. That said company shall not allow the transfer of any share or shares of stock, except by resolution of the board of directors, until all the instalments have been paid, and if any stockholder shall omit for the space of six months, to pay any instalment which may have been called for, the directors of the company may either declare the share or shares of stock on which the instalment or instalments are unpaid, as aforesaid, to be forfeited, or may at their option, bring suit to recover the said instalment or instalments with interest at the rate of ten per centum per annum, against the person or persons appearing by their books, to be the owner or owners thereof. *Transfer of stock*

6. That the dividends of so much of the profits of said company as shall appear advisable to the directors, shall be declared in the months of January and July of each year, and be paid at the office of said company any time after ten day's notice from the time of declaring the same, but said dividends shall in no case exceed the amount of the net profits of said company, so that the capital stock shall never be thereby impaired, and in case the directors shall declare a dividend exceeding the amount of the net profits and thereby impair the capital stock, they shall be held individually liable for all such excess. *Dividends.*

7. That the said railway company shall be, and they are hereby required to lay the track of their said road of such a guage as to be most convenient for the use of carriages and buggies passing over the said road, and in all cases the carriage or vehicle following the car shall have the right to the track, and the carriage or vehicle coming in the opposite direction, shall be required to turn off of the track. *Guage of road.*

8. That if any person or persons shall wilfully break, remove, destroy, or injure any part of said railway or cars, carriages, station houses, or any buildings or property of said company, or shall, without the consent of said company, wilfully and unnecessarily obstruct or impede the passage on or over the said railway or any part thereof, the person or persons so offending shall forfeit and pay for every such offence, the sum of five dollars to the said company, but no such suit shall be brought unless commenced within thirty days after such offence shall have been committed, and the person or persons so offending, shall be liable, in addition to said penalty, *Offences.* *Limitation of suit.*

to action or actions at the suit of the said railway company, for any loss or damage occasioned by his or her or their acts as aforesaid.

Grades of streets 9. The said railway company shall not alter the grade of any street over which the said road passes, without the consent of the corporation through which the said street passes, having first been obtained to the said alteration, and the said railway company shall keep so much of the said streets in perpetual and good repair, as are used by the said company, from the distance of two feet on the outer side of one rail to a like distance on the outer side of the opposite rail of their said track, at the proper expense and charge of the said company, and the said company shall in no case use locomotive engines on said road without first obtaining the consent of the corporation through which the said railway passes.

Powers of corporations through which the said road passes. 10. That the corporations through which the said railway passes shall have power to establish such regulations in said railway, as may be requisite for the purpose of paving, repairing, grading, culverting and laying gas and water pipes, in and along the streets used by said company, and to prevent obstructions thereon; and

Tax. the corporation of the city of Wheeling may assess and collect a tax on the cars used by said company on the streets of said city, of a sum to be agreed on between the said company and the said city: provided, the said sum so assessed be not more than at the rate of $25 per annum, for each car used in the said streets; and the town of South Wheeling, may, in like manner, assess and collect a tax on the cars run through the streets of said town, of a sum not exceeding the rate of $5 a year for each car used in said streets.

Fare. 11. That no greater fare shall be charged upon the line of said road, east of the Ohio river, than ten cents per passenger, and no greater fare on the line of said road passing over the bridges and island, to the limit of the state of Virginia, than fifteen cents per passenger, and the said railway company are hereby authorized and empowered to transfer and carry to and from any and all points upon the line of said road, baggage, parcels and packages, at such rates as may be fixed by the board of directors of the company.

Commencement. 12. This act shall be in force from its passage.

CHAP. 47.—An ACT making an appropriation to rebuild a bridge over Stony River on the North Western Turnpike, in Hardy county.

Passed January 30, 1863.

1. Be it enacted by the General Assemby of Virginia, That the sum of thirty-two dollars, be, and is hereby appropriated out of

ACTS OF THE GENERAL ASSEMBLY. 37

any money in the treasury, not otherwise appropriated, to be ex- *Appropriation for rebuilding bridge over Stony river.*
pended by the board of public works for the purpose of rebuilding
the bridge over Stony river on the north western turnpike in Hardy
county.

2. This act shall be in force from its passage. *Commencement.*

CHAP. 48.—An ACT appropriating the Capitation Tax for the year 1862, for Educational purposes.

Passed January 30, 1863.

1. Be it enacted by the General Assembly, That the auditor of *Auditor to ascertain amount of capitation tax paid into the treasury for the years 1861 and 1862.*
public accounts do ascertain as soon as practicable, the amount of
capitation tax paid into the treasury for the years 1861 and 1862,
from the several counties and the cities and towns having corporation courts, and set apart the same to the credit of the literary fund
for the purposes of education and primary and free schools.

2. The said auditor shall cause the amount thus ascertained by
him to have been paid into the treasury, from each county, city, or
town having a county or corporation court, to be paid to and ap- *How fund to be applied.*
plied in every such county, city, or town, to the purposes of education in the manner now prescribed by law, and to existing claims
lawfully due from said fund for educational purposes, in the order
of time in which they were audited and allowed according to law.

3. The money in the treasury of the state, as well as all moneys
that may hereafter come into the treasury, derived either from fines, *What constitute the fund.*
forfeitures or dividends on stocks standing in the name of the literary fund, as well as interest on loans due the same, shall constitute part of the general fund of the state: provided however, that *Proviso.*
the general assembly, when the cities, towns and counties of the
state are in condition to use the same, be refunded and distributed
as the general assembly shall think just and proper.

4. This act shall be in force from its passage. *Commencement.*

CHAP. 49.—An ACT staying the collection of certain debts.

Passed January 30, 1863.

1. Be it enacted by the General Assembly of Virginia, That
no writ of *fieri facias*, order, or other process issued under any *No writ of fieri facias, or other process to issue.*
judgment or decree heretofore rendered by any court of this commonwealth, or justice of the peace, nor that may be hereafter ren-

ACTS OF THE GENERAL ASSEMBLY.

dered by any such court or justice, shall be placed in the hands of any sheriff or other officer to be levied, while this act shall re-

No sales to be had under any deed of trust heretofore executed.

main in force, nor shall there be any sales under any deed of trust heretofore recorded, without the consent of all the parties thereto, nor under any decree or judgment since rendered or that may be hereafter rendered, except as otherwise herein provided for, and in

Levy.
Property to be returned to owner.
Lien.

any case where a levy has been made previous to the passage of this act, the property so levied on shall be returned to the owner, and the judgment, under which the levy was made, shall be a lien on all the property both personal and real, of the debtor, and shall have priority over all other judgments as to the personal property of such debtor.

2. Be it further enacted, that any person may sue for any debt, and maintain any action at law or in equity, and proceed to judgment therein, and any judgment, execution, order or decree now issued or rendered, or that may hereafter be rendered, shall, in addition to the provisions of chapter one hundred and eighty-six and

Lien on real and personal estate.

one hundred and eighty-eight of the Code of 1860, constitute a lien on all the estate, both personal and real of the judgment debtor, from and after the docketing of any such judgment, as is provided for in the third and fourth sections of chapter one hundred and

What is included

eighty-six of the Code of 1860. This provision shall include all judgments whether rendered by justices of the peace or courts of this commonwealth.

3. In all debts or liabilities accruing before the 26th day of July, 1861, the debtor is required, upon the demand of the creditor, to

Debtor required to pay the interest on demand.

pay the interest due thereon within six months after demand thereof and upon failure therein, may be proceeded against as if this act had never been passed.

4. Be it further enacted, that in all cases where a lien has been acquired by judgment or decree before any court or justice of the peace of this commonwealth, or by any deed of trust, the creditor may proceed against the debtor, and enforce the collection of his

When the debtor may enforce the collection of his debt.
Proviso.

debt, interest and costs, in the same manner as if this act had never been passed: provided however, that such creditor, his assignee, personal representative, agent, or attorney, shall first file with the clerk of the court or justice of the peace, as the case may be, an affidavit that the affiant believes that the debtor in such case intends to remove or has removed his effects out of the county where the judgment or decree was rendered, or in which the same is docketed, or if a deed of trust, out of the county where the same is recorded, or that he is fraudulently removing, or disposing of the same, so that it will not be forthcoming and liable to the payment of the judgment, decree, or deed of trust, as the case may be, at the expiration of this act. But the debtor may contest the credi- *When debtor may contest creditor's right to proceed against him.* tor's right to such proceedings, and upon a motion by the debtor to quash the same upon the grounds that he was not removing, nor did intend so to remove his effects or fraudulently dispose of the same, as alleged by the creditor, the court or justice of the peace before whom such motion is made, shall, in determining such controversy be governed by the same rules of law that they are now governed by in determining cases of attachments: provided however, *Proviso.* that no sale or barter by any person in the ordinary transaction of his business or calling, shall be deemed to be fraudulent, within the meaning of this section.

5. Be it further enacted, that nothing herein contained shall be construed so as to interfere with or abridge the law now in force in *Exceptions.* relation to attachments and acts of detinue and trover, nor in relation to injuries or torts, nor in relation to actions of ejectment and unlawful entry and detainer, nor in relation to the prosecution of criminal offences and the collection of fines, taxes, licenses, county levies, and all debts due the commonwealth, but the same may be proceeded in, as now provided for by law, nor shall this act apply to sheriffs, constables, or other public officers, either to the state, counties, corporations, or individuals, nor to attornies at law, for moneys collected, nor to debts contracted after the 26th day of July, 1861, nor to debts nor deeds of trust executed after the said 26th day of July, 1861; but payment of and sales under the same may be enforced and proceeded in as if this act had not been passed; nor shall the time during which this act is in force be computed in any case in which the statute of limitations may come in question: provided however, that the benefits of this act *Proviso.* shall not extend to any person who shall, after the passage thereof, be engaged in levying war against the government of the United States or against the reorganized government of Virginia, adhering to and giving aid and comfort to their enemies, and any judgment creditor may issue his execution and proceed to the collection of such judgment upon making affidavit before the clerk of the court wherein such judgment is recorded or before the justice by whom the judgment was rendered, that such debtor is so engaged, which execution may be quashed at the instance of the defendant upon his showing that the allegations upon which it issued, were untrue.

6. This act shall be in force from the first day of February, *Commencement. Expiration.* 1863, and shall expire on the first day of January, 1864.

CHAP. 50.—An ACT changing a place of voting in the county of Morgan.

Passed January 31, 1863.

Place of holding elections discontinued.
1. Be it enacted by the General Assembly, That the separate elections heretofore authorized to be holden at the houses of Unger and Humes, in the county of Morgan, be and the same are hereby abolished, and in lieu thereof the elections hereafter to be held for said places of voting, shall be held at the house of Bazzoc Shockeys, in said county of Morgan, at which election precinct all persons qualified by law to vote, may vote.

New place of voting.

Commencement. 2. This act shall be in force from its passage.

CHAP. 51.—An ACT allowing certain claims out of any money derived from assessment of fines for the non-performance of military duty, under the order of the Governor by his proclamation dated September 9th, 1862.

Passed January 31, 1863.

1. Be it enacted by the General Assembly of Virginia, That the auditor of public accounts be required to pay any claims of any county when properly certified by a regimental court, for expenses incurred by said county in organizing and drilling the militia in September, October and November, 1862, under the order of the Governor by his proclamation dated September 9th, 1862, out of any money that may come into the treasury from the assessment of fines against persons in said county for non-performance of military duty in September, October and November, 1862, under the order of the Governor by his proclamation dated September 9th, 1862.

Expenses of militia.

Commencement. 2. This act shall be in force from its passage.

CHAP. 52—An ACT in reference to the troops raised within the boundaries of the proposed State of West Virginia.

Passed January 31, 1863.

Troops of West Virginia.
1. Be it enacted by the General Assembly of Virginia, That the troops raised within the boundaries of the proposed state of West Virginia, and now in the service of the United States, shall, when the said proposed state becomes one of the United States, be and become to all intents and purposes the volunteer militia of the state of West

ACTS OF THE GENERAL ASSEMBLY. 41

Virginia in the service of the United States, and shall be regulated, governed and officered in the same manner as if they had been raised and organized under the constitution and laws of the state of West Virginia.

2. This act shall be in force from its passage. Commencement.

CHAP. 53.—An ACT changing the place of holding Elections in Pleasants county.

Passed January 31, 1863.

1. Be it enacted by the General Assembly, That the election precint heretofore existing at Pine Grove Meeting House in the second magisteral district, in the county of Pleasants, be and the same is hereby abolished, and in lieu thereof the elections shall be held at T. D. Gorrell's store, in Hebron, in the district and county above named, which is hereby made a lawful place of voting. Election precinct abolished. Election precinct established.

2. This act shall be in force from and after its passage. Commencement.

CHAP. 54.—An ACT giving the consent of the State of Virginia to the county of Berkeley being admitted into and becoming part of the State of West Virginia.

Passed January 31, 1863.

WHEREAS, by the constitution for the state of West Virginia, rati- Preamble. fied by the people thereof, it is provided that additional territory may be admitted into and become part of said state with the consent of the legislature thereof, and it is represented to the general assembly that the people of the county of Berkeley are desirous that said county should be admitted into and become part of the said state of West Virginia; now, therefore,

1. Be it enacted by the General Assembly, That polls shall be opened and held on the fourth Thursday of May next at the several places for holding elections in the county of Berkeley, for the purpose of taking the sense of the qualified voters of said county on the question of including said county in the state of West Virginia. Polls to be opened.

2. The poll books shall be headed as follows, viz: "Shall the county of Berkeley become a part of the state of West Virginia," and shall contain two columns, one headed "aye" and the other "no," and the names of those who vote in favor of said county becoming part of the state of West Virginia shall be entered in the first col- Poll books.

umn, and the names of those who vote against it shall be entered in the second column.

3. The said polls shall be superintended and conducted according to the laws regulating general elections, and the commissioners Superintendance superintending the same at the court-house of the said county, shall within six days from the commencement of the said vote examine and compare the several polls taken in the county, strike therefrom any votes which are by law directed to be stricken from the same, and attach to the polls a list of the votes stricken therefrom and the reasons for so doing. The result of the polls shall then be ascertained, declared and certified as follows: The said commissioners shall make out two returns in the following form, or to the following Form of returns. effect:—"We, commissioners for taking the vote of the qualified voters of Berkeley county on the question of including the said county in the state of West Virginia, do hereby certify that polls for that purpose were opened and held the fourth Thursday of May, in the year 1863, within said county pursuant to law, and that the following is a true statement of the result as exhibited by the poll books, viz: for the county of Berkeley becoming part of the state of West Virginia, —— votes; and against it, —— votes. Given under our hands this —— day of ————, 1863;" which returns written in words, not in figures, shall be signed by the commissioners; one of the said Where said returns are to be filed. returns shall be filed in the clerk's office of the said county, and the other shall be sent under the seal of the secretary of this commonwealth within ten days from the commencement of the said vote, and the governor of this state, if of opinion that the said vote has been opened and held, and the result ascertained and certified pursuant to law, shall certify the result of the same under the seal of this state to the governor of the said state of West Virginia.

4. If the governor of this state shall be of opinion that the said polls cannot be safely and properly opened and held in the said county Governor may postpone opening of polls. of Berkeley on the fourth Thursday of May next, he may by proclamation postpone the same, and appoint in the same proclamation or by one to be thereafter issued another day for opening and holding the same.

5. If a majority of the votes given at the polls opened and held When said county may become part of the new State. pursuant to this act be in favor of the said county of Berkeley becoming part of the state of West Virginia, then shall the said county become part of the said state of West Virginia when admitted into the same with the consent of the legislature thereof.

Commencement. 6. This act shall be in force from its passage.

CHAP. 55.—An ACT for the relief of Solomon Parsons, of the county of Tucker.

Passed February 3, 1863.

1. Be it enacted by the General Assembly, That the auditor of public accounts, be, and is hereby directed to issue his warrant in favor of Solomon Parsons, for the sum of twenty-seven dollars and fifty-four cents, to be paid out of any moneys in the treasury, not otherwise appropriated; said sum of money being the amount paid into the treasury by said Solomon Parsons as taxes upon license for the years 1861-2, which license, owing to repeated raids of rebel soldiers into the county of Tucker, he has been prevented from using. *Auditor to issue his warrant.*

2. This act shall be in force from its passage. *Commencement.*

CHAP. 56.—An ACT changing a place of voting in the county of Jackson.

Passed February 3, 1863.

1. Be it enacted by the General Assembly, That the place of voting known as the Sandyville precinct, in the county of Jackson, be and the same is hereby changed to the house of Warrin Reeds in said county, and that hereafter it shall be lawful to open polls for voting at the house of said Warrin Reeds instead of the Sandyville precinct. *Change of place of voting.*

2. This act shall be in force from its passage. *Commencement.*

CHAP. 57.—An ACT to regulate the election of officers by the Council of the city of Wheeling.

Passed February 3, 1863.

1. Be it enacted by the General Assembly of Virginia, That all officers which now are, or hereafter may be, required by acts of the legislature to be elected by the council of the city of Wheeling, shall be elected by joint ballot of the first and second branches of said council, a quorum of each branch being present, or in such other mode as shall be prescribed by the ordinances of said city. *All officers to be elected by joint ballot.*

2. This act shall be in force from its passage. *Commencement.*

ACTS OF THE GENERAL ASSEMBLY.

CHAP. 58.—An ACT to confer upon the President of the second branch of the Council of the City of Wheeling the power to administer oaths.

Passed February 3, 1863.

President to administer oaths.
1. Be it enacted by the General Assembly of Virginia, That the president of the second branch of the council of the city of Wheeling, for the time being, shall be, and he is hereby constituted a justice of the peace so far as administering oaths is concerned within the limits of the said city: provided that he shall not sit as a justice in the county court of Ohio county.

Commencement.
2. This act shall be in force from its passage.

CHAP. 59.—An ACT for the relief of Henry Snider.

Passed February 3, 1863.

Henry Snider released from fine.
1. Be it enacted by the General Assembly of Virginia, That Henry Snider, of Marshall county, be and he is hereby released from the payment of a fine of one hundred dollars, assessed against him by the county court of said county of Marshall at the November term, 1859, of said county court.

Commencement.
2. This act shall be in force from its passage.

CHAP. 60.—An ACT to provide for the payment of certain volunteers in companies A and B, of the 10th Virginia Regiment Volunteer Infantry, for services rendered not paid for.

Passed February 3, 1863.

Auditor authorized to pay certain volunteers.
1. Be it enacted by the General Assembly, That the auditor of public accounts, be, and the same is hereby authorized to pay out of the treasury, out of any moneys not otherwise appropriated, a sum sufficient to pay, at the rates of thirteen dollars per month, to James Smallridge, William Smallridge, and William Hyre of company B, 10th Virginia regiment volunteer infantry; also, to James Pickens and Thomas Cunningham of company A, of said regiment, for actual services rendered as state volunteers, from the time they were sworn into the state service to the time when the same were mustered out of the service by an officer of the United States, because of over age, receiving no pay for faithful services rendered.

Proviso.
2. Provided, that on applications for pay by any of said volunteers for any such service rendered, that the same shall be required (by either themselves, heirs, agents, or attorneys, as the case may

be,) to furnish satisfactory evidence to the governor, of the time and faithful performance rendered in the volunteer service of the state by each volunteer so applying for pay, and when the governor shall be satisfied, upon such evidence as may be produced, that any of the said volunteers are entitled to pay for service so rendered, that he may order the same to be paid in accordance with the provisions of this act, and said order shall be a sufficient voucher to the auditor for any such moneys paid by him.

3. This act shall be in force from its passage. Commencement.

CHAP. 61.—An ACT imposing a Tax on Dogs.

Passed February 3, 1863.

1. Be it enacted by the General Assembly, That it shall be lawful for the several county courts of this commonwealth, all the magistrates being first summoned for this or any other purpose, and a majority being present, to levy a tax on dogs owned or kept in their respective counties; and it shall be the duty of the commissioners of the revenue, provided the county courts shall so order, of the respective counties, to list annually all dogs in their districts and make return thereof to said courts, and the names of the owners arranged in alphabetical order, at the May or June terms of said courts. To impose a tax on dogs.
Proviso.

2. Every house-keeper may be allowed one dog free of tax, and for every additional dog there shall be a tax of not less than one nor more than two dollars. Housekeepers allowed one dog.

3. The taxes so levied shall be paid by the persons respectively in whose names the dogs shall be listed; and the owner or occupier of any house, lot, or plantation, about or upon which any dog may be kept or permitted to remain, shall be deemed, for the purposes of this act, the owner of such dog or dogs. By whom taxes are to be paid.

4. If any person shall conceal his dog or send him to any place for the purpose of avoiding the tax, he shall pay a fine of five dollars, recoverable before any justice of the peace for the county, with costs. Fine.

5. Every person when called on by the commissioner of his district, shall disclose on oath the number of dogs owned by him, or kept or permitted to remain about any house, or upon any lot or plantation in his occupancy or under his control; and such oath shall be administered by the commissioner. Number of dogs to be disclosed on oath.

6. The taxes imposed upon dogs under this act, shall be collected and accounted for by the sheriffs of the respective counties, as county How taxes collected and accounted for.

ACTS OF THE GENERAL ASSEMBLY.

levies are by law directed to be collected and accounted for; and to this end it shall be the duty of the courts on or before the July term of each year to cause a list to be delivered to the sheriffs, containing the names of all persons charged with a dog tax, and showing the amount assessed severally against each.

Duty of courts.

Lists.
7. The courts of the several counties shall cause a list or lists containing the names of all persons failing to pay the dog tax assessed against him to be delivered to the constables of the several districts in which they respectively reside, with the number of dogs listed to, and the amount of tax assessed severally against each, for which such constable shall give his official receipt to the court, and it shall be the duty of the constable upon receiving such list forthwith to make a demand upon the delinquent party for the payment of such tax, and upon the failure to pay over the tax that may be assessed against such delinquent party, it shall be the duty of the constable forthwith to search out and kill every dog in respect to the tax on which the owner shall be delinquent. Any person who shall conceal a dog for the purpose of avoiding the provisions of this section shall pay a fine of ten dollars, recoverable before any justice in and for the county, with costs.

Demand.

Duty of constables.

Fine.

8. Every such sheriff or constable receiving such lists as are mentioned in the two preceding sections, shall settle and pay over, on or before the first day of January of each year, to the persons appointed to receive the same, all moneys due from the said tax on dogs of the preceding year, after deducting the delinquents and commission of seven and a half per centum; and they shall make due return to the county courts of the March term of each year, of the manner in which they have discharged their duties respecting the same, and shall be liable for the tax assessed upon every dog enumerated in such lists as they shall fail to return a satisfactory account of to the court.

Returns, how to be made.

Fee for killing dogs.
How paid.
9. The constable shall receive fifty cents for every dog they may kill under the provisions of the eighth section, to be paid out of the dog tax, or county levy, and they and their securities shall be liable on their official bonds, upon motion in said courts, for any money received by them, or which they may be liable to pay by virtue of this act.

Fee for labor in listing and furnishing copies of lists.
10. The commissioners of the revenue and clerks shall be allowed a reasonable compensation for their labors in listing and furnishing copies of list to the sheriffs and constables, to be fixed by the courts of the several counties.

How money arising from dogs disposed of.
11. The money arising from the said tax on dogs, shall, after defraying the expenses of the execution of the said law, so far as

ACTS OF THE GENERAL ASSEMBLY. 47

may be necessary, shall, by an order of the county court, upon satisfactory evidence be applied to the payment of the owners of all sheep killed by dogs: provided however, that applicants applying **Proviso.** to be paid for sheep so killed, shall be required to state under oath, that the same was not killed by their own dogs; the money remaining shall be applied to county purposes.

12. This Act shall be in force from its passage. **Commencement.**

CHAP. 62.—An ACT to amend and re-enact an act passed the 28th day of March, 1861, amending and re-enacting the seventh section of the one hundred and sixty-fifth chapter of the Code.

Passed February 3, 1863.

1. Be it enacted by the General Assembly of Virginia, That the **Section seven of** seventh section of the one hundred and sixty-fifth chapter of the **chapter 165 amended and re-** Code of Virginia be amended and re-enacted so as to read as follows: **enacted.**

"§7. Such attorney in any county or corporation court shall be allowed by the court, such sum as it deems reasonable for public service (for which no other fee or reward is allowed by law) which shall be chargeable to such county or corporation, and in the circuit court shall be allowed by it, where the attorney has no annual salary, such sums as it deems reasonable, not exceeding in one year, one hundred and fifty dollars in the circuit court of the county and city of Norfolk, and one hundred dollars in any other circuit court, except that additional allowances may be made by such courts for services rendered at special terms; and except that the attorney for the circuit court of the city of Richmond shall hereafter receive annually the sum of five hundred dollars; and except also, that the attorneys for the commonwealth for the circuit court of Ohio county shall hereafter receive annually the sum of two hundred and fifty dollars, to be paid half yearly as the present allowance is directed to be paid."

2. All acts and parts of acts coming in conflict with the provisions of this act, are hereby repealed. **All acts or parts of acts inconsistent with this act repealed.**

3. This act shall be in force from its passage. **Commencement.**

CHAP. 63.—An ACT for the relief of the heirs of William P. Rathbone, deceased.

Passed February 3, 1863.

WHEREAS, William P. Rathbone, late of Wood county, deceased, **Preamble.** omitted from his last will any devise or bequest of the bulk of his estate, whereby the same has descended and passed, under the provisions of the one hundred and twenty-third chapter of the Code of Virginia, to his surviving children and the descendants of his deceased children in parcenary; and whereas, a portion of his real estate so undevised, consists of one equal undivided third part of about six hundred acres of land, situated in Wirt county, on the Little Kanawha river and Burning Spring run, whereof two equal undivided third parts were by said decedent in his life time, granted and conveyed to his sons J. Castelli Rathbone and John V. Rathbone, who have since by deeds, duly recorded in Wirt county, bearing date on the second day of January in the year one thousand eight hundred and fifty-four, made partition as between themselves, so that each is now owner of two equal undivided third parts of a designated moiety of the said six hundred acres of land; and whereas, the said land is the principal locality of petroleum yet discovered in this state, and during the life time of the said decedent he joined with his sons above named, in several leases of oil rights, having still about eighteen years to run, on various parts of the said land, which consists of detached parcels, and it is unknown whether extensive portions of the said land, on which no wells have yet been bored, will yield petroleum, or in what quantities; and whereas, the heirs of the said decedent comprise children, grandchildren and great grand-children, some of the second, and all of the last being minors under the age of twenty-one years, and residing in the state of New York and in England; and whereas, a partition in kind of the said land cannot be equitably made, and a sale of the same for the purpose of effecting a partition would be injurious to the interests of all the said heirs, and particularly of said minors, and unless some arrangement can be speedily made by which the petroleum and other products of the said land can be availed of, all of them will remain without any considerable increase therefrom and the public be deprived of the benefits of a valuable production; and whereas, the said John V. Rathbone heretofore agreed to grant and convey to Johnson N. Camden and other parties hereinafter named, one-half of his undivided two-thirds of a moiety of the said land, all of whom, except the said Camden and John J. Jackson, Jr., are now in the service of the so-called confederate states, or voluntarily residing within their actual jurisdiction and yielding them allegiance, the greater portion of their agreed purchase money being unpaid, and their purchase subject to sale under their vendor's lien; and whereas, the adult heirs of the said decedent, including the said J. Castelli Rathbone and John V. Rathbone, and the guardian and father and grand-father of the said minor heirs, act-

ACTS OF THE GENERAL ASSEMBLY.   49

ing on this behalf so far as he may, as to their respective interests in the said land, and the said J. Castelli Rathbone as to his undivided two-thirds of a moiety of the said land, have agreed to form and constitute a joint stock company for the better management and improvement of their interests and estate in said land: and whereas, the courts cannot grant adequate relief in the premises, Therefore,

1. Be it enacted by the General Assembly of Virginia, That James Cook, John R. Murdock, and Hugh P. Dills, are hereby appointed commissioners to set off by metes and bounds, and to allot to the said John V. Rathbone and his said vendees, to-wit: Johnson N. Camden, John J. Jackson, jr., William J. Bland, William L. Jackson, Gideon D. Camden, R. S. Andrews and B. H. Byrne, having regard to quantity and quality and estimated value, two equal undivided third parts of that moiety of the above described six hundred acres of land, his interest in which the said J Castelli Rathbone partitioned, granted and released to the said John V. Rathbone, as aforesaid, and in a like manner set off and allot to the Rathbone Petroleum company, hereby incorporated, the residue of the said six hundred acres of land. *Commissioners.*

2. Upon the completion of the partition and allotment hereby authorized and directed, the said commissioners shall cause to be prepared a sufficient deed or deeds granting and assuring to the parties to whom said land shall be so partitioned and allotted, their respective portions and parcels thereof with proper covenants of warranty and relinquishment of dower; upon the execution and acknowledgment for record whereof by or on part of all the adult heirs of the said decedent, their wives and husbands, and by the commissioner first named in the preceding section, who is also appointed a commissioner for this latter purpose for and on behalf of all minor heirs of the said decedent, and also for and on behalf of the vendees of the said John V. Rathbone, their heirs and assigns, to-wit: Johnson N. Camden, John J. Jackson, jr., William J. Bland, William L. Jackson, Gideon D. Camden, R. S. Andrews, and B. H. Byrne, the partition and allotment hereby authorized and directed shall be binding in law and equity on all the parties thereto, but without prejudice to the rights of any other person or persons. *Commissioners to make deeds.*

3. The said heirs, to-wit: J. Castelli Rathbone, John V. Rathbone, Samuel B. Rathbone, William Van Allen Rathbone, Ellen S. Frost (wife of Daniel Frost), Rathbone Van Winkle, Godwin Van Winkle, Mary V. Blackford (wife of J. Graham Blackford), Hoffman Atkinson, Edward S. Atkinson, Jerome Gill Atkinson, George M. Atkinson, John H. Morrison, Mary A. Morrison, and Richard

4

ACTS OF THE GENERAL ASSEMBLY.

R. Morrison, their respective executors, administrators and assigns, are hereby incorporated into a joint stock company by the name of the Rathbone Petroleum Company, for the purpose of raising to the surface, manufacturing, preparing for and transporting to market, selling and otherwise disposing of the mineral and other products of their interest and estate in the said land, and may devise and lease for terms not exceeding twenty-years, any parts or parcels of their said land, with the privilege to their lessee of boring for and obtaining therefrom petroleum and other products thereof, reserving the rents in kind or otherwise. The said company shall be governed by the provisions of the fifty-sixth and fifty-seventh chapters of the Code of Virginia (excepting the thirty-second and the first clause of the thirty-fifth section of the latter,) so far as the same are applicable and are not inconsistent with any provisions of this act.

Rathbone Petroleum Company incorporated.

4. The capital stock of the said company shall consist of one thousand and fifty shares of one hundred dollars each, which shall be apportioned and assigned as follows, to-wit: to the said J. Castelli Rathbone, six hundred shares; to the said John V. Rathbone, Samuel B. Rathbone, William Van Allen Rathbone, and Ellen S. Frost, each seventy-five shares; to the said Rathbone Van Winkle, Godwin Van Winkle, and Mary V. Blackford, each twenty-five shares; to Hoffman Atkinson, fifteen shares, and to John P. Atkinson, who is hereby appointed a trustee for the purposes of this act, the residue of the said shares, to have and hold the same in trust for his minor children and grand-children until they respectively attain the age of twenty-one years, and then to assign and transfer to each the shares owned by him or her, or in the event of the death of either before attaining such age, then to assign and transfer the shares of such decedent to his or her heirs, executors or administrators, that is to say: he shall hold in trust as aforesaid, for the use and benefit of his children, the said Edward S. Atkinson, Jerome Gill Atkinson, and George M. Atkinson, each fifteen shares, and of his grand-children, the said John A. Morrison, Mary A. Morrison, and Richard R. Morrison, each five shares, and the said company shall have power from time to time, by a majority of two-thirds of the votes cast at any annual or special meeting of the stockholders thereof, to increase their capital stock by the addition of so many shares as the same majority may agree to allow and issue for any portion or portions of the said six hundred acres of land, not theretofore owned by them, which may be duly granted and conveyed to them, and may hold and use the land so acquired, for the purposes of this incorporation. At all general meetings and

Capital stock.

ACTS OF THE GENERAL ASSEMBLY. 51

elections each stockholder may in person or by proxy, cast one vote for each share of stock owned by him or her, and the said trustee may in like manner, cast one vote for each share of stock held by him in trust, as aforesaid.

5. For the purpose of facilitating the transportation of their productions and manufactures to market, the said company may procure, own and use such steam and other vessels and vehicles as they may deem necessary; they may also subscribe for, purchase and own such amount of the capital stock of any company incorporated for the purpose of improving the navigation of the Little Kanawha river, or for constructing a railroad or turnpike to or from the land owned by them, as may be authorized by two-thirds of the votes cast at any annual or special meeting of the stockholders, but the said company shall not purchase or hold any other land than is herein authorized, except so much as may be necessary for sites for their manufactories, work-shops, warehouses, yards for the storeage of their products, and wharves for the use of the vessels owned or employed by them. *Said company authorised to use steam and other vessels and vehicles necessary for their business*

6. This act shall be in force from its passage, but is to be subject to be altered, amended or repealed by any future legislature. *Commencement. May be altered, amended or repealed.*

CHAP. 64.—An ACT imposing Taxes for the Support of the Government.

Passed February 3, 1863.

TAXES.

1. Be it enacted by the General Assembly, That the taxes on the persons and subjects in this act mentioned, or required by law to be listed or assessed, shall be yearly, as follows: *Taxes.*

On Lands and Lots.

On tracts of lands and lots, with the improvements thereon, not exempt from taxation, thirty cents on every hundred dollars value thereof; and herein shall be included all tracts of lands and lots, with the improvements thereon, not exempt from taxation, of incorporated joint stock companies, savings institutions and insurance companies. *Amount of taxation on real property not exempt*

On Personal Property.

2. On all of the personal property, moneys and credits required by law to be listed and not exempt from taxation, except slaves, thirty cents on every hundred dollars value thereof; and herein shall be included all the capital invested or used in any manufac- *Tax on personal property not exempt, and on monies and credits.*

turing business except gas companies, where the assessment shall be on the value of such property invested or employed in any trade or business except agriculture, for which no license is required, and all the personal property and moneys of incorporated joint stock companies, except the moneys and personal property that constitute part of the capital of the banks, and except the moneys and personal property of savings institutions and insurance companies which have declared dividends within one year preceding the first day of February; and the words "moneys and credits" shall be construed to include all moneys and credits owned by any resident in this state, whether such moneys or credits are within or without the state.

On Slaves.

On slaves. 3. On every slave over twelve years of age, whether exempted from county levy in consequence of bodily infirmity or not, ninety cents; and herein shall be included all slaves over twelve years of age, owned or hired by any company, institutions or persons whatsoever.

On Free Negroes.

On free negroes. 4. On every male free negro who has attained the age of twenty-one years, sixty cents.

White Males.

White males. 5. On every white male inhabitant who has attained the age of twenty-one years, sixty cents.

On Public Bonds.

Public bonds. 6. On the interest or profit which may have been received by any person, or converted into principal so as to become an interest bearing subject, or otherwise appropriated, within the year next preceding the first day of February of each year, arising from bonds and certificates of debt of this or any other state or country, or of any corporation created by this or any other state, whether the stock of such company be exempt from taxation or not, five per centum.

Dividends of Savings Institutions and Insurance Companies.

Dividends of savings institutions and insurance companies 7. On the dividends declared within the year preceding the first day of February, by savings institutions and insurance companies, to be paid by such institutions and companies into the treasury respectively, five per centum.

On Incomes and Fees.

Incomes and fees 8. On the income or fees received during the year preceding the first day of February of each year, in the consideration of the discharge of any office or employment in the service of the state, or in consideration of the discharge of any office or employment in the service of any corporation, or in the service of any company, firm, or person, except where the service is that of a minister of the gospel, three-fourths of one per centum if the same be more than two hundred and fifty dollars and not more than five hundred dollars, one per centum if the sum be more than five hundred dollars and not more than a thousand dollars; and one and a half per centum if the sum be over one thousand dollars. The tax payable under this section by an officer of the government receiving a salary out of the treasury, shall be deducted at the time the salary is audited and paid. *Tax payable by officer of government to be deducted at time of payment of salary.*

Bridges and Ferries.

9. On the yearly rent or annual value of toll bridges and ferries other than those toll bridges and ferries exempt by their charter from taxation, four and a half per centum. *Toll bridges and ferries.*

ON LICENSES.
Ordinaries.

10. The tax on licenses shall be as follows:

On a license to keep an ordinary or house of public entertainment, thirty dollars; and if the yearly value of such house and furniture exceeds one hundred dollars and is less than two hundred dollars, the tax shall be forty dollars; and if the yearly value thereof exceeds two hundred dollars, there shall be added to the last mentioned sum twelve per centum on so much thereof as exceeds two hundred dollars. *Ordinaries and houses of public entertainment.*

Private Entertainment and Houses of Public Resort.

11. On a lincense to keep a house of private entertainment or a private boarding house, five dollars; and if the yearly value of such house and furniture exceeds fifty dollars and is less than one hundred dollars, the tax shall be ten dollars. If the yearly value thereof exceeds one hundred dollars, there shall be added to the last mentioned sum, eight per centum on so much thereof as exceeds one hundred dollars. But no house shall be deemed a private boarding house with less than five boarders. *Houses of private entertainment and public resort.*

Eating Houses.

12. On every license to keep a cook-shop or eating-house, fifteen dollars; and in addition thereto twelve per centum on so much of the yearly value thereof as exceeds one hundred dollars. *Cook shops and eating houses.*

Bowling Alleys and Billiard Tables.

13. On every license permitting a bowling alley or saloon to be kept for a year, fifty dollars; provided that where there is more than one such alley kept in any one room, fifteen dollars each shall be charged for the excess over one. *Bowling alleys.*

14. And on every license permitting a billiard table to be kept for a year, one hundred dollars; provided that where there is more then one such table kept in any one room, fifty dollars each shall be *Billiard tables.*

charged·for the excess over one table: provided that if such billiard table, bowling alley or saloon is not kept open more than four months in any one year, the taxes thereon shall be only one-half of these rates.

Bagatelle Tables.

Bagatelle tables. 15. On every license permitting a bagatelle or other like table to be kept for one year or any less time, twenty dollars for the first, and if more than one, ten dollars for the second, and five dollars for each additional table kept in the same house.

Livery Stables.

Livery stables. 16. On every license to a keeper of a livery stable, seventy-five cents for each stall thereof; and therein shall be included as stalls, such space as may be necessary for a horse to stand, and in which a horse is or may be kept.

Distilleries.

Distilleries. 17. On every license to the proprietor of a distillery, if a beginner, the tax shall be fifteen dollars; and if said distillery is to be kept in operation as much as four months in the year, the tax shall be twenty-five dollars; if for six months, thirty dollars; if for nine months, forty-five dollars; if for a longer time than nine months, seventy-five dollars; and if such distillery has been kept in operation as much as four months in the year next preceding the time of obtaining such license, the proprietor thereof shall pay, in addition to the tax imposed on beginners, four-tenths of one per centum on the amount of sales of such distillery for the twelve months next preceding the time of obtaining such license.

Merchants.

Merchants. 18. On every license to a merchant or mercantile firm, where a specific tax is to be paid, forty-five dollars: provided that if the capital employed by said merchant or firm be shown by affidavit to be less than five hundred dollars, the tax to be paid shall be eight dollars; but this provision shall not authorize any such person to

Sale of liquors. sell wine, ardent spirits or a mixture thereof; and when the tax is in proportion to the sales, if the table sales shall be under one thousand and one dollars, the tax shall be fifteen dollars; if one thousand and one and under fifteen hundred dollars, eighteen dollars; if fifteen hundred dollars and under twenty-five hundred dollars, twenty-four dollars; if twenty-five hundred dollars and under five thousand dollars, thirty-six dollars; if five thousand dollars and under ten thousand dollars, fifty-seven dollars; if ten thousand and under fifteen thousand dollars, seventy-two dollars; if fifteen thousand and under twenty thousand dollars, eighty-four dollars; if twenty thousand and under thirty thousand dollars, one hundred and five dollars; if thirty thousand and under fifty thousand dollars, one hundred and fifty-six dollars; if over fifty thousand dollars; eight dollars for every ten thousand dollars excess over the said sum of fifty thousand dollars.

Merchants' Permission to Sell Liquor. License to sell liquor.

19. And in every case in which the license to a merchant or mercantile firm includes permission to sell wine, ardent spirits or a mixture thereof, porter, ale or beer, by wholesale and retail, or by retail only, if such merchant or firm (commencing business for the first time) sell by wholesale and retail, an additional tax of seventy-five dollars; and if by retail only, thirty dollars; and if such license be to a merchant or mercantile firm to continue the privilege of selling wine, ardent spirits or a mixture thereof, porter, ale or beer, if by wholesale and retail, or by retail only, the tax shall be three-fourths of one per centum on the amount of such sales for the year next preceding the time of obtaining said license, in addition to the specific tax imposed on beginners; but such sales shall not be estimated in ascertaining the amount of a merchant's license.

Merchant Tailors, Lumber Merchants, Ice and Fuel Dealers.

20. Merchant tailors, lumber merchants, dealers in coal, ice or wood, shall obtain license as merchants, and be assessed and taxed thereon as other merchants are by the preceding sections of this act, and shall be subject to like penalties for conducting such business without a merchant's license. Merchant tailors lumber merchants and fuel dealers.

Commission or Forwarding Merchants, Tobacco Auctioners or Ship Brokers.

21. The tax on every license to a commission merchant, forwarding merchant, tobacco auctioner or ship broker, shall be thirty dollars, if commencing business; and if to continue such business after the same has been carried on for a year, the tax on such lincese shall be one and one-half per centum on the amount of commissions received; and this tax shall be in addition to such tax as may be imposed on a license to such merchant or firm to sell any goods, wares or merchandize. Commission merchants, tobacco auctioneers or ship brokers.

Auctioneers.

22. On every license to an auctioneer or vendue master commencing business, twenty dollars; and if the place of business be in a town containing a population of three thousand inhabitants, twenty-five dollars; if the population exceeds three thousand, an additional tax of twelve dollars for every thousand persons above that number; and at that rate for any fractional excess less than one thousand; and said specific tax shall in no case exceed three hundred dollars. On every license to an auctioneer who deals exclu- Auctioneers.

sively in real-estate, one hundred and eighty-eight dollars, and he shall have the right to sell real-estate at auction or otherwise. On every license to an auctioneer or vendue master to continue the business after the same has been carried on for a year, three-fourth of one per centum on the amount of taxable sales of such auctioneer or vendue master, but in no case shall the tax on such sales exceed seven hundred and fifty dollars; provided the tax to be paid by auctioneers for the sale of molasses and sugar, shall in no case exceed four hundred dollars for such sales; but the tax on sales of other articles shall not be affected by this provision.

Sample Merchants.

Sample merch'ts   23. On every license to a person selling goods by sample, card or otherwise, except at some storehouse or place of trade, one hundred and fifty dollars; but such sales made at such storehouse shall subject the person doing business at such storehouse to the tax required to be paid by a merchant.

Patent Rights and Patent Medicines.

Patent rights.   24. On every license to sell or barter patent rights, twenty dollars; patent, specific or quack medicines, if by wholesale, forty dollars; if by retail only, twenty dollars, unless he have a merchant's license.

Agents for Renting Houses and Hiring Negroes.

Agents for renting houses.   25. On every license to a person engaged as agent for the renting of houses, twenty dollars.

Agents for hiring negroes.   26. On every license to a person engaged as agent for the hiring of negroes, forty dollars.

Stallions.

Stallions and asses.   27. On every license to the owner of a jackass or stallion, for the service of which compensation is received, twice the amount of such compensation, when the charge is for such service by the season; and where such services are for less than a season, then twice what a commissioner may judge to be a reasonable charge therefor. The tax, however, in no case to be less than ten dollars.

Theatrical Performances, Sale of Refreshments in Theatres.

Theatrical performances.   28. On every license permitting theatrical performances, public show, exhibition, concert or other performance in a public theatre or elsewhere, six dillars each week of such performances, notwithstanding the owner of the place of exhibition shall have paid the license tax above required.

Refreshments in theatres.   29. On every license permitting the sale of refreshments in a theatre during such performances, seventy-five dollars for each place of sale, and no abatement shall be made if the privilege be exercised for a period less than one year.

ACTS OF THE GENERAL ASSEMBLY. 57

Public Rooms and Shows.

30. On every license permitting the proprietor or occupier of any public room fitted for public exhibitions, to use the same for such purposes for a year, fifteen dollars, if such room be in a town of less than five thousand inhabitants; thirty dollars if in a town of more than five thousand and less than ten thousand inhabitants; and forty-five dollars in all other towns; and in addition to these rates there shall be added to said license tax thirty cents on every hundred dollars value of such rooms or buildings, provided such rooms and buildings are not otherwise assessed. *Public rooms.*

31. On every license permitting any public show, exhibition or performance, except where held in a room licensed under the provisions of the preceding section of this act, if in a corporate town, or if within five miles thereof, for each time of performance, ten dollars; if elsewhere, five dollars; and for every exhibition of a circus, if within a corporate town, or within five miles thereof, thirty dollars; if elsewhere, fifteen dollars; and for every exhibition of a menagerie, if within a corporate town, or five miles thereof, thirty dollars; if elsewhere, fifteen dollars. All such shows, exhibitions and performances, whether under the same canvas or not, shall be construed to require a separate license therefor, and upon any such shows, exhibitions, and performance being concluded, so that an additional fee for admission be charged, the same shall be construed to require an additional license therefor. *Shows.*

Porter, Ale and Beer.

32. On every license to sell by retail, porter, ale or beer, when in a city or town the population of which is over eight hundred, fifteen dollars; and all other places, ten dollars, and if they continue for more than one year, an additional tax of three-fourths of one per centum on the amount of taxable sales. *Porter, Ale or Beer.*

Stock Brokers.

33. On every license to a broker who deals exclusively in stocks, one hundred and eighty-eight dollars; and he shall thereupon have the right to sell the said stocks at auction or otherwise. *Stock Brokers.*

Bank Note Brokers.

34. On every license to a broker employing a capital of ten thousand dollars, or a less sum, two hundred dollars; on all sums over ten thousand dollars, two per centum on the capital employed. *Bank Note Brokers.*

Foreign Insurance Companies.

35. On every license to an agent or sub-agent of any insurance company not chartered by this state, fifty dollars; and in addition thereto a tax of one-half of one per centum on the whole amount of premiums received and assessments collected by such agent or sub-agent or company within the state as prescribed by law. *Foreign Insurance companies*

Physicians, Dentists and Lawyers.

Physicians, Dentists and lawyers 36. On every license to a physician, surgeon or dentist, five dollars; and on every license to an attorney-at-law, five dollars. If the yearly income derived from the practice of any such callings or profession during the year next preceding the time of obtaining such license shall exceed four hundred dollars, there shall be an additional tax on the excess, of three-fourths of one per centum, and this income shall be included in the license tax.

Daguerrean Artists.

Daguerrean Gallery. 37. On every license to the owner of a daguerrean or such like gallery by whatsoever name it may be known or called, if in a city or incorporated town of less than one thousand inhabitants, ten dollars; if more than one thousand inhabitants, thirty dollars; if elsewhere, eight dollars; and if the yearly income derived from the practice of said art exceeds five hundred dollars in any county, city or town, an additional tax of one and one-half per centum on such excess for the year next preceding the time of obtaining such license; and such tax shall be imposed whether an artist perform in a gallery or not.

Express Companies.

Express Companies. 38. On every license to a person or company carrying on an express business for compensation, forty dollars; and in addition thereto, every such company shall make a return to the auditor of public accounts on the fifteenth day of January and July in each year of the total receipts of such company, on account of its operations within the state of Virginia within the six months preceding the first day of January and July of each year. Such returns shall be verified by the oaths of the agent and chief officers of such company, at its principal office or offices in this state, in the manner and according to the form prescribed by the said auditor, whether collected within or without the state. Such express companies shall pay on the total receipts so reported, a tax of four tenths per centum, except for the transportation of bank notes, for which the tax shall be one eighth of one per centum upon the amount of bank notes transported over one hundred miles at any one time, except notes sent by the banks and sheriffs of this commonwealth, and for failure to make such report or pay such tax, a penalty of six hundred dollars shall be imposed on the company so failing, to be recovered as other penalties are: provided, however, that no license to carry on the express business shall authorize any such company to do the business of a broker. Such license shall give the privilege throughout the state.

39. No express company shall pay any tax on bank notes for-

ACTS OF THE GENERAL ASSEMBLY.   59

warded for any resident citizen of this commonwealth, unless he be a broker dealing in bank notes.

Bank Dividends.

40. On the dividends declared by any bank incorporated by this state, the tax shall be five per centum upon the amount thereof, to be paid into the treasury by the bank. If the dividend be that of a bank incorporated elsewhere, the tax shall be five per centum upon the amount thereof, to be assessed and collected as other taxes. *Bank dividends.*

On Suits.

41. When any original suit, attachment or other action is commenced in a circuit, county or corporation court, there shall be a tax of fifty cents; if it be an appeal, writ of error, or supersedeas in a district court, two dollars, and if in the court of appeals, two dollars and fifty cents. *On suits.*

On Seals.

42. When the seal of a court, of a notary public, or the seal of the state is annexed to any paper, except in those cases exempted by law, the taxes shall be as follows, for the seal of the state, two dollars; for the seal of a court or a notary public or any other seal, fifty cents; for any other seal, one dollar and fifty cents, except in cases of protests of bills or notes for one hundred dollars or smaller sums, in which cases the tax shall be fifty cents, and herein shall be included a tax on a scroll annexed to a paper in lieu of an official seal. *Seals.*

On Wills and Administrations.

43. On the probate of every will or grant of administration, there shall be a tax of one dollar. *Wills and administrations.*

Deeds.

44. On every deed admitted to record, whether the same has been recorded before or not, which is admitted to record, there shall be a tax of one dollar. *Deeds,*

Internal Improvement Companies.

45. Every railroad company or canal company shall hereafter report quarterly, on the 15th day of March, June, September and December in each year, to the auditor of public accounts, the number of passengers transported, and the aggregate number of miles traveled by them within this commonwealth, the gross amount received by such company for transportation of freight over such road or canal, or any part thereof, during the quarter of the year next preceding the first day of the month in which such report is made. Such company, whose road or canal is only in part within the commonwealth, shall report as aforesaid such portion only of such amount received for the transportation of freight, as the part of *Internal Improvement companies.*

ACTS OF THE GENERAL ASSEMBLY.

the said road or canal which is within this commonwealth, bears to the whole of such road or canal.

46. Such statement shall be verified by the oaths of the president and the superintendent of transportation, or other proper officer. Every company failing to make such report, shall be fined five hundred dollars. At the time of making such report, the company shall pay into the treasury, for every passenger transported, a tax at the rate of one mill for every mile of transportation of each of such passengers, and a tax of one-third of one per centum of such gross amount received for the transportation of freight. Every such company paying such taxes, shall not be assessed with any tax on its lands, buildings, cars, boats or other property which they are authorized by law to hold or have. But if such company fail to pay such taxes at either of the terms specified therefor, then its lands, buildings, cars, boats and other property shall be immediately assessed under the directions of the auditor of public accounts, by any person appointed by him for the purpose, at its full value, and a tax shall at once be levied thereon as on real estate and other property, to be collected by any sheriff whom the auditor may direct, and such sheriff shall distrain and sell any personal property of such company, and pay such taxes into the treasury within three months from the time when such assessment is furnished to him.

Sale of Horses for profit.

Sale of horses, mules, asses, jennets, cattle, sheep, or hogs.
47. On every license to buy or sell for others on commission or for profit, horses, mules, asses and jennets, cattle, sheep or hogs, ten dollars.

Carriages and other Vehicles.

On Carriages and other vehicles.
48. On every license to sell carriages, buggies, barouches, coaches, gigs, wagons, and such like vehicles, manufactured out of this state, forty dollars in each county or corporation.

Sale of Slaves.

Sales of slaves.
49. On every license to buy or sell for others on commission or for profit, slaves, ten dollars; and on the yearly income derived from such business, an additional tax of one per centum.

Commencement.
50. This act shall be in force from its passage.

CHAP. 65.—An ACT appropriating the Public Revenue for the fiscal year 1862–3, and a part of the fiscal year 1863–4.

Passed February 4, 1863.

Appropriation of the Public Revenue for the fiscal
1. Be it enacted by the General Assembly, That the surplus of all appropriations made prior to the 30th September, 1862, and any

ACTS OF THE GENERAL ASSEMBLY. 61

and all moneys in the treasury not otherwise appropriated at the close of the fiscal year ending September 30th, 1862, as well as all moneys that shall come into the public treasury, from and after the 30th day of September, 1862, to the 31st day of December, 1863, shall constitute a general fund and be appropriated for the fiscal year 1862–3, and for the months of October, November and December, in the fiscal year 1863–4, as follows: *year 1862-3, and a part of the fiscal year 1863-4.*

To expenses of general assembly for the extra session commencing on the 4th day of December, 1862, including pay of officers, printing, stationery, &c.,	$17,000 *Expenses of General Assembly.*
To salaries of officers of civil government,	12,500 *Salaries of officers of civil government.*
To expenses of the judiciary, including salaries of the judges, attorneys of the commonwealth, mileage, &c.,	10,000 *Judiciary.*
To defray expenses of criminal charges, including witnesses, jurors, and jailor fees,	6,000 *Criminal charges.*
To contingent expenses of the courts of the commonwealth,	5,000 *Contingent expenses of Courts.*
To expenses of convicts in jail or other places, including transportation,	1,500 *Convicts.*
To expenses of lunatics in jails or in asylums in other states, including transportation and salary, in part, of superintendent of asylum at Williamsburg,	5,000 *Lunatics.*
To salary of adjutant general,	1,200 *Adjutant General*
To public printer,	1,500 *Public Printer.*
To expenses of elections,	200 *Elections.*
To pay of commissioners of the revenue,	10,000 *Commissioners of Revenue.*
To expenses of coroner's inquests,	100 *Coroner's Inquests.*
To pay of clerks in auditor's office,	1,500 *Clerks in Auditors office.*
To pay of clerks in treasurer's office,	200 *Clerks in Treasurer's office.*
To pay of clerks in adjutant general's office,	625 *Clerks in Adjutant General's office.*
To pay of janitor for executive's office,	400 *Janitor.*
To contingent expenses of the offices of the auditor, treasurer and secretary of the commonwealth, including stationery, fuel, postage, printing, books, &c.,	2,500 *Contingent expenses of Auditor, Treasurer, and Secretary of the Commonwealth.*
To contingent expenses of the adjutant general's office,	500
To civil contingent fund,	15,000 *Civil contingent fund.*
To expenses of the convention which is to assemble in the city of Wheeling on the 12th day of February, 1863, including the pay and mileage of its members, the compensation of its officers, its printing, stationery, fuel, and other necessary expenditures, and also including the expenses of holding any elections which may be ordered by said convention,	7,000 *Expenses of Convention.*
To salary of vaccine agent,	500 *Vaccine agent.*

ACTS OF THE GENERAL ASSEMBLY.

Principal of Linsley Institute. To the principal of Linsley Institute for the use of the building during the extra session of the general assembly, commencing December 4, 1862, two dollars and fifty cents per day, ... 157 50

Sick, wounded & dead soldiers belonging to Virginia regiments. To defray expenses of transporting sick, wounded and dead soldiers belonging to Virginia regiments who are unable to pay their transportation from the fated field or hospital, to their homes, said fund to be at the disposal of the governor of the commonwealth, . . . 2,000

Sergeant-at-Arms of House of Delegates. To sergeant-at-arms of the house of delegates for expenses incurred in preparing the hall for the use of the house of delegates, including cleansing and replacing carpets, removing and replacing furniture, and use or hire of same, 75 00

Mrs. Tompkins. To pay Mrs. Tompkins for extra labor in the hall of the house, ... 50 00

Collecting and taking care of the arms of the Commonwealth. To expense of collecting together, putting in order and taking care of the arms of this commonwealth, to be allowed by the auditor, upon the certificate of the governor, 1,000

Clerk of Senate. To the clerk of the senate, in addition to his present compensation, ... 50 00

Who not entitled to claim or receive any money by virtue of this act. 2. Be it further enacted, that no judge, attorney for the commonwealth, or other officer in state service, who has not taken the oath required by the ordinance for the re-organization of the state government, or who, after taking and subscribing such oath, shall, by any overt act or by writing or speaking, support and uphold or attempt to support and uphold the usurped government at Richmond, or the pretended government of the so-called confederate states, shall not be entitled to claim or receive any money by virtue of this act.

3. Be it further enacted, that the unexpended surplus of all appropriations made in the first section of this act, remaining in *What moneys shall constitute a general fund.* the treasury on the first day of January, 1864, and all moneys that may remain in the treasury, by virtue of the provisions of the second section of an act passed February 4, 1863, entitled "an act making an appropriation to the proposed new state of West Virginia," as also all moneys now due from the United States to the state for expenses incurred for military purposes, (when collected and paid into the treasury by the governor,) shall constitute a general fund to defray such expenses authorized by law, as are not herein particularly provided for, and to defray the current expenses of the commonwealth for that portion of the fiscal year ending Sept. 30, 1864, not herein specifically provided for.

Commencement. 4. This act shall be in force from its passage.

CHAP. 66.—An ACT authorizing the Governor to arrest disloyal persons as hostages.

Passed February 4, 1863.

WHEREAS, it is known to the General Assembly, That evil dis- Preamble. posed persons and others under the influence and orders of the assumed rebel government, have made it a practice (and recently, too,) entered West Virginia and seized and carried away citizens into the so-called southern confederacy, and there have detained and imprisoned them without cause, and unless this system of kidnapping be promptly checked, such conduct will continue and increase to the manifest oppression of our loyal citizens, for remedy whereof,

1. Be it enacted by the General Assembly of Virginia, That the governor of this commonwealth is hereby authorized and requested in all cases of the seizure of the persons of loyal citizens of this state by any parties acting under the authority of the so-called Who to be seized and held as hostages. southern confederacy, the pretended state government at Richmond or other military organizations acting in sympathy or concert with them, or either of them, to seize and hold as hostages for the safe rendition of such person or persons so seized and held, so many persons of known disloyal sentiments as in his discretion may be necessary to effect said rendition.

2. This act shall be in force from its passage. Commencement.

CHAP. 67.—An ACT to amend and re-enact the seventh section of the Ordinance passed June the 19th, 1861, entitled "An Ordinance to authorize the apprehending of suspicious persons in time of war.

Passed February 4, 1863.

1. Be it enacted by the General Assembly, That the seventh Section seven of the Ordinance section of the ordinance passed the 19th day of June, 1861, enti- passed June 19, 1861, amended tled "an ordinance to authorize the apprehending of suspicious per- and re-enacted. sons in time of war," be amended and re-enacted so as to read as follows:

"§7. The powers vested in the governor by this ordinance shall be exercised only upon satisfactory evidence of the necessity of such arrest, based upon oath or affirmation.

2. This act shall be in force from its passage. Commencement.

ACTS OF THE GENERAL ASSEMBLY.

CHAP. 68.—An ACT transferring to the proposed State of West Virginia, when the same shall become one of the United States, all this State's interest in property, unpaid and uncollected taxes, fines, forfeitures, penalties and judgments, in counties embraced within the boundaries of the proposed State aforesaid.

,Passed February 3, 1863.

Transfer of property.
1. Be it enacted by the General Assembly of Virginia, That all property, real, personal and mixed, owned by or appertaining to this state, and being within the boundaries of the proposed state of West Virginia, when the same becomes one of the United States, shall thereupon pass to and become the property of the state of West Virginia, and without any other assignment, conveyance, transfer or delivery than is herein contained ; and shall include among other things not herein specified, all lands, buildings, roads and other internal improvements, or parts thereof situated within the said boundaries, and now vested in this state, or in the president and directors of the board of the literary fund, or the board of public works thereof, or in any person or persons, for the use of this state to the extent of the interest and estate of this state therein; and shall also include the interest of this state, or of the said president and directors, or of the said board of public works, in any parent bank or branch doing business within the said boundaries; and all stocks of any other company or corporation, the principal office or place of business whereof is located within the said boundaries standing in the name of this state or of the said president or directors, or of the said board of public public works, or of any person or persons, for the use of this state.

Taxes, fines, forfeitures. &c., &c., transferred.
2. Be it further enacted, That all unpaid and uncollected arrearages of taxes on lands, town lots, property tax, capitation tax, license tax, militia fines, fines imposed by courts, forfeitures and penalties, belonging to the state in the hands of sheriffs, collectors or individuals, in any or all of the counties embraced within the boundaries of the proposed state of West Virginia, as also all bonuses on the capital stock of any bank, taxes on the dividends declared by any bank, savings institution or insurance company; dividends on stock owned by the state, or by the board of public works, or the president and directors of the board of the literary fund, in any bank, bridge or other corporation in any one of the counties aforesaid; also taxes on seals, deeds, wills, writs and other legal processes due from the clerks of the courts, notaries public or the secretary of the commonwealth; taxes on passengers and tonnage due from railroad companies, taxes on bank notes or other property transported by

express companies within the counties aforesaid; also all fines, forfeitures and penalties incurred by railroads, express companies or other parties or persons within the counties aforesaid; also all judgments, decrees or penalties incurred by officers of the state, railroad or express companies, or other persons before or since the re-organization of the state government at the city of Wheeling; also all suits and their results now pending in the name of the board of public works, or of the president and directors of the board of the literary fund in any court of any of the counties aforesaid; also all taxes on lands, town lots, property tax, capitation tax, license tax, assessed in the counties aforesaid, and due the state for the year 1863, in the hands of officers of the state or individuals, together with all the rights of the state, or of the board of public works, or of the president and directors of the board of the Literary fund to any and all moneys and claims in the counties aforesaid that may not be specifically mentioned in this act, but that rightfully belong to the state or corporations for the use of the state, shall be the property of the state of West Virginia, when the same shall become one of the United States.

3. It shall be the duty of all sheriffs or collectors of the public revenue, also of all presidents or other officers of railroad, express, bridge or internal improvement companies, presidents and other officers of banks, savings banks and insurance companies, clerks of courts, notaries public, the secretary of the commonwealth, and of individuals owing or having money in their hands due the state, or the board of public works, or the president and directors of the board of the literary fund, in any of the counties aforesaid, to pay the same into the treasury of the state of West Virginia, when the same shall become one of the United States. *What moneys to be paid into the treasury of West Virginia.*

4. Be it further enacted, For the purpose of carrying this act into effect, that suits may be brought in the name of this commonwealth for the use of the state of West Virginia, when it becomes one of the United States, on any bond or claim which shall pass to or become the property of the State of West Virginia by virtue of this act. *Suits to be brought in the name of the state of West Virginia.*

5. Be it further enacted, That if the appropriations and transfers of property, stocks and credits provided for by this act take effect, the state of West Virginia shall duly account for the same in the settlement hereafter to be made with this state: provided that no such property, stocks and credits shall have been obtained since the re-organization of the state government. *State of West Virginia to account with this state. Proviso.*

6. It shall be the duty of the auditor of public accounts, the secretary of state, the treasurer, and the adjutant general of this *Duty of officers of State.*

66   ACTS OF THE GENERAL ASSEMBLY.

commonwealth to procure fit and proper blank books for the purpose, and cause to be transcribed therein true copies of all such records, official acts, orders, minutes and memoranda, and like copies of original papers upon which any such official action was based, which from its locality or general state interest appertains to and will be useful and advantageous to the state of West Virginia; and the officers aforesaid shall severally certify to the governor of this commonwealth the correctness of their respective copies ; and it shall be

Duty of Governor. the duty of the governor to certify to all whom it may concern, the official character of such officers so certifying under the great seal of this commonwealth, and deliver all such copies to the governor of West Virginia, when his election is officially declared, for the use of said state of West Virginia.

Commencement. 7. This act shall take effect when the proposed state of West Virginia shall become one of the United States.

CHAP. 69.—An ACT providing for placing a part of the Maryland and Ohio Turnpike under the supervision of the County Court of Marion.

Passed February 4, 1863.

A portion of the Maryland & Ohio Turnpike placed under the supervision of the County Court of Marion county. 1. Be it enacted by the General Assembly of Virginia, That so much of the Maryland and Ohio turnpike as runs between the town of Mannington in the county of Marion and to the point at which the said pike crosses the dividing line between the counties of Marion and Wetzel, be placed and the same is hereby placed under the supervision and control of the county court of the said county, and the court of the said county is hereby empowered to lay off the said pike into precincts, and to place the same under supervisors, and the said road, when so precincted and placed under supervisors, shall be worked and controlled as county roads are worked and

Proviso. controlled by law: provided, that nothing herein contained shall be construed so as to transfer any interest which the state may have in the said pike.

Commencement. 2. This act shall be in force from its passage.

CHAP. 70.—An ACT directing in what manner the Commissioners of the Revenue in certain counties shall return their books.

Passed February 4, 1863.

1. Be it enacted by the General Assembly of Virginia, That the commissioners of the revenue of this state residing in any of the

counties within the limits of the proposed state of West Virginia, after having completed their books and assessments of license for the year 1863, and after having furnished the sheriffs of the said counties with the commissioners books and license lists, shall return the commissioners books and license lists now required by law, to be returned to the auditor of the state, to the auditor of the said proposed state of West Virginia, if the said state shall then be organized and admitted as one of the states of the United States. If at the time when these books are properly returnable to the auditor, the proposed state of West Virginia shall not be admitted as one of the United States, the commissioners of the revenue for the counties aforesaid, shall then return their books as now required by law. *Directing how Commissioners of the Revenue in certain counties shall return their books.*

2. This act shall be in force from its passage. *Commencement.*

CHAP. 71.—An ACT to amend and re-enact the second and third sections of the third chapter of the Code of 1860.

Passed February 3, 1863.

1. Be it enacted by the General Assembly of Virginia, That the second and third sections of the third chapter of the Code of 1860 be amended and re-enacted so as to read as follows: *The second and third sections of chapter three of the Code of 1860 amended and re-enacted.*

"§2. Whenever a citizen of this state, by deed in writing executed in the presence of and subscribed by two witnesses, and by them proven in the court of the county or corporation where he resides, or by open verbal declaration made in such court and entered of record, shall declare that he relinquishes the character of a citizen of this state and shall depart out of the same, such person shall, from the time of such departure, be considered as having exercised his right of expatriation so far as regards this state and shall thenceforth be deemed no citizen thereof.

"§3. When any citizen of this state, being twenty-one years of age, shall reside elsewhere, and in good faith become the citizen of some other state of this union, or the citizen or subject of a foreign state or sovereign, he shall not, while the citizen of another state, or the citizen or subject of a foreign state or sovereign, be deemed a citizen of this state; and any citizen of this state who shall, after the passage of this act, voluntarily levy war against the United States, or who shall adhere to the enemies of the same, or give them aid and comfort, or who shall, by writing or speaking, profess allegiance or fidelity to the so-called confederate states of America, or who shall resist or oppose by violence, or who shall by writing or

ACTS OF THE GENERAL ASSEMBLY.

speaking instigate others to resist or oppose by violence, the government of Virginia as reorganized by the convention which assembled at Wheeling on the 11th day of June, 1861, shall be considered as having expatriated himself so far as regards this state, and shall thenceforth be deemed no citizen thereof."

Commencement. 2. This act shall be in force from its passage.

CHAP. 72.—An ACT making an appropriation to the proposed new State of West Virginia when the same shall become one of the United States.

Passed February 4, 1863.

Appropriation to the State of West Virginia. 1. Be it enacted by the General Assembly of Virginia, That the sum of one hundred and fifty thousand dollars, be, and is hereby appropriated to the state of West Virginia out of moneys not otherwise appropriated, when the same shall have been formed, organized and admitted as one of the states of the United States.

Additional appropriations. 2. Be it further enacted, that there shall be, and hereby is appropriated to the said state of West Virginia when the same shall become one of the United States, all balances, not otherwise appropriated, that may remain in the treasury, and all moneys not otherwise appropriated, that may come into the treasury up to the time when the said state of West Virginia shall become one of the United States:

Proviso. provided, however, that when the said state of West Virginia shall become one of the United States, it shall be the duty of the auditor of this state, to make a statement of all the moneys that up to that time, have been paid into the treasury from counties located outside of the boundaries of the said state of West Virginia, and also of all moneys that up to the same time, have been expended in such counties, and the unexpended surplus of all such moneys shall remain in the treasury and continue to be the property of this state.

The act passed May 14, 1862, repealed. 3. Be it further enacted, that the act passed May 14, 1862, making an appropriation of one hundred thousand dollars to the state of West Virginia, be, and the same is hereby repealed.

Commencement. 4. This act shall be in force from its passage.

CHAP. 73.—An ACT for the relief of Greenville Harrison.

Passed February 4, 1863.

Auditor directed to issue his warrant in favor of Greenville Harrison. 1. Be it enacted by the General Assembly of Virginia, That the auditor of public accounts be and hereby is directed to issue his

ACTS OF THE GENERAL ASSEMBLY. 69

warrant in favor of Greenville Harrison for the sum of $92,75, to be paid out of any moneys in the treasury not otherwise appropriated, such sum being the amount justly due to said Harrison for services rendered by him as commissioner of the revenue for the county of Cabell in making out property books for the year 1862, which books were forcibly taken from said Harrison on the 3d day January, 1863, by rebel soldiers. Commencement.

2. This act shall be in force from its passage.

CHAP. 74.—An ACT for the relief of Theodore Davis.

Passed February 2, 1863.

1. Be it enacted by the General Assembly of Virginia, That Theodore Davis, be, and he is hereby released from the payment of a fine of two hundred dollars, imposed upon him by the circuit court of Doddridge county, at the spring term of 1862, for an assault upon one Jacob Trough, with intent to maim, disfigure and disable him, the said Trough. Released from payment of a fine.

2. This act shall be in force from its passage. Commencement.

CHAP. 75.—An ACT for the relief of James G. West.

Passed February 4, 1863.

1. Be it enacted by the General Assembly, That the auditor of public accounts be and hereby is directed to issue his warrant in favor of James G. West for the sum of fourteen hundred and forty dollars and thirty cents, to be paid out of any moneys arising from suit or suits pending against the Baltimore and Ohio Railroad Company for damages done to the Maryland and Ohio Turnpike Road, and that the said James G. West and his securities be, and they are hereby released from the bond of said James G. West as contractor on the Maryland and Ohio Turnpike Road. Auditor directed to issue his warrant in favor of James G. West.
Released from bond.

2. This act shall be in force from its passage. Commencement.

CHAP. 76.—An ACT authorizing the Auditor to regulate the compensation of Commissioners of the Revenue in certain cases.

Passed February 4, 1863.

1. Be it enacted by the General Assembly, That the auditor of public accounts is hereby authorized and directed to allow commis- Compensation allowed Commissioners of the Revenue.

ACTS OF THE GENERAL ASSEMBLY.

sioners of the revenue in all counties, except those in which the said commissioners receive a fixed compensation, such additional compensation for the year 1863 as will raise the salary of said commissioners of the revenue to an amount not exceeding that paid them for the year 1862.

Commencement. 2. This act shall be in force from its passage.

CHAP. 77.—An ACT to incorporate the Little Kanawha Navigation Company.

Passed February 4, 1863.

Who authorized to open books of subscription.
1. Be it enacted by the General Assembly, That it shall be lawful to open books, under the superintendence of John V. Rathbone, P. G. Van Winkle, J. N. Camden, James Cook, Moses Kinchelo, Daniel Wilkinson, E. C. Hopkins, Jonathan Weaver, Charles Chaddoc, John Wear, and James A. Williamson, or any three of them, at Parkersburg, in the county of Wood, at Newark, Elizabeth, and Rathbone, in the county of Wirt, and at Glenville, in the county of Gilmer, for receiving subscriptions to the capital stock of the company hereby incorporated for the purpose of improving the navigation of the Little Kanawha river and its branches.

Capital stock.
Name of company.
2. The capital stock of said company shall consist of four thousand shares of twenty-five dollars each, and whenever five hundred shares are subscribed the subscribers, their executors, administrators and assigns, are hereby incorporated by the name of the Little Kanawha Navigation Company, and shall be governed by the provisions of the fifty-sixth, fifty-seventh and sixty-first chapters of the Code of Virginia, so far as the same are applicable and not inconsistent with this act. The county courts of Wood, Wirt, Ritchie, and Gilmer counties shall have the power to subscribe. At all general meetings and elections each stockholder may in person, or by proxy, cast one vote for every share of stock owned by him.

Number of votes authorized to be cast by stockholders.
Improvements.
3. The said company shall have power to improve the navigation of said river, and of Hughes' river, by locks and dams, sluices, canals, or other usual modes of improvement or by the combination of any two or more of them. They shall commence their improvements at or near the mouth of said river, and prosecute the same toward the head, so far as may be deemed practicable, and their resources will permit, and may in like manner improve Hughes' river so far up the same as they may deem proper, when their main improvement has reached the mouth thereof; they may enter and condemn lands for the purposes of their improvements, under the

provisions of the said fifty-sixth chapter of the Code of Virginia, and shall have the benefit of all or any acts declaring the said river a navigable highway; they may charge and receive such tolls for the use of their improvement as may be fixed by the board of public works, or by law.

Tolls.

4. The said company shall have power to borrow money from time to time, not exceeding in the aggregate the amount of their capital stock; to issue their bonds or other proper securities for the same, and to pledge their works and property by mortgage or deed of trust for the payment thereof and of the interest to accrue thereon, but in the event of a sale under such mortgage or deed of trust, all bonds or notes then outstanding, issued in payment for work done or materials furnished on or for their improvement, and so expressed to be on their face, shall be first paid out of the proceeds of any such sale.

Power to borrow money.

5. The said company shall commence the said improvement within two years after the passage of this act and complete the said improvement up the said Kanawha river to the mouth of the west fork of said river, within eight years after the passage of this act, and if the said company fails to complete the improvement from the said west fork to Glenville, in Gilmer county, within ten years after the passage of this act, the right as a company to said Kanawha river, shall be forfeited and no longer to exist above the mouth of the said west fork of the Kanawha, but shall have the right granted in this act to continue as a company from the mouth of the said Kanawha to the mouth of the said west fork.

In what time improvements to be commenced.

6. This act shall be in force from its passage.

Commencement.

CHAP. 78.—An ACT giving consent to the admission of certain counties into the new State of West Virginia, upon certain conditions.

Passed February 4, 1863.

1. Be it enacted by the General Assembly of Virginia, That at the general election on the fourth Thursday of May, one thousand eight hundred and sixty-three, it shall be lawful for the voters of the district composed of the counties of Tazewell, Bland, Giles, and Craig, to declare by their votes whether said counties shall be annexed to and become a part of the new state of West Virginia; also, at the same time, the district composed of the counties of Buchanan, Wise, Russell, Scott, and Lee, to declare by their votes whether the counties of the said last named district shall be an-

Lawful for the voters of Tazewell, Bland, Giles and Craig to declare by their votes whether said counties shall be annexed to West Virginia.

Also the counties of Buchanan, Wise, Russell, Scott, and Lee.

ACTS OF THE GENERAL ASSEMBLY.

<small>Also the counties of Alleghany, Bath and Highland.</small>
nexed to and become a part of the state of West Virginia; also, at the same time, the district composed of the counties of Alleghany, Bath, and Highland, to declare by their votes, whether the counties of such last named district shall be annexed to and become a part of the state of West Virginia; also, at the same time, the dis-
<small>Also the counties of Frederick and Jefferson.</small>
trict composed of the counties of Frederick, and Jefferson, or either of them, to declare by their votes, whether the counties of the said last named district shall be annexed to and become a part of the state of West Virginia; also, at the same time, the district compo-
<small>Also the counties of Clarke, Loudoun, Fairfax, Alexandria and Prince William.</small>
sed of the counties of Clarke, Loudoun, Fairfax, Alexandria, and Prince William, to declare by their votes, whether the counties of the said last named district shall be annexed to and become a part of the state of West Virginia; also, at the same time, the district
<small>Also the counties of Shenandoah, Warren, Page & Rockingham.</small>
composed of the counties of Shenandoah, Warren, Page, and Rockingham, to declare by their votes, whether the counties of the said last named district shall be annexed to and become a part of the state of West Virginia; and for that purpose there shall be a poll
<small>Polls to be opened.</small>
opened at each place of voting in each of said districts, headed
<small>Consent.</small>
"For Annexation," and "Against Annexation." And the consent of this general assembly is hereby given for the annexation to the said state of West Virginia of such of said districts or either of them, as a majority of the votes so polled in each district may determine: provided, that the legislature of the state of West Virginia shall also consent and agree to the said annexation, after which all jurisdiction of the state of Virginia over the districts so annexed shall cease.

<small>Duty of Governor</small>
2. It shall be the duty of the governor of the commonwealth to ascertain and certify the result as other elections are certified.

<small>If election cannot be held on day mentioned, Governor to issue his proclamation ordering such election.</small>
3. In the event the state of the country will not permit, or from any cause, said election for annexation cannot be fairly held on the day aforesaid, it shall be the duty of the governor of this commonwealth, as soon as such election can be safely and fairly held and a full and free expression of the opinion of the people had thereon, to issue his proclamation ordering such election for the purpose aforesaid, and certify the result as aforesaid.

<small>Commencement.</small>
4. This act shall be in force from its passage.

CHAP. 79.—An ACT for the relief of Alexander Hay.

Passed February 5, 1863.

<small>The sale of the Alexandria and Washington railroad made a lawful sale.</small>
1. Be it enacted by the General Assembly of Virginia, That the sale of the Alexandria and Washington railroad made on the tenth

day of April, eighteen hundred and sixty-two, and the purchase of the same by Alexander Hay and his associates, be, and hereby is made a lawful sale, and shall not in any wise be effected by the law "staying the collection of certain debts," passed July 26th, 1861, and amended and re-enacted February 8th, 1862, and again extended December 22d, 1862; and said sale shall be deemed valid, of full force and effect as if said law had never been passed. *Not effected by the law "staying the collection of certain debts."*

2. This act shall be in force from its passage. *Commencement.*

CHAP. 80.—An ACT amending and re-enacting section eight of an Act passed January 31st, 1863, entitled "An Act imposing taxes for the support of the Government.

Passed February 5, 1863.

1. Be it enacted by the General Assembly, That section eight of an act passed January 31st, 1863, entitled "an act imposing taxes for the support of the government," be amended and re-enacted so as to read as follows: *Section eight of an Act passed Jan. 31st, 1863, amended re-enacted.*

"§8. On the income, salary or fees received during the year ending the first day of February of each year in consideration of the discharge of any office or employment in the service of the state, or in consideration of the discharge of any office or employment in the service of any corporation, or in the service of any company, firm or person, except where the service is that of a minister of the Gospel, three-fourths of one per centum upon so much thereof as exceeds five hundred dollars.

The tax on a salary payable under this section by an officer of the government receiving the same out of the treasury, shall be deducted at the rate chargeable on the annual salary on the amount drawn from the treasury at the time the salary is audited and paid; and fees or other income of such officer shall be listed and assessd by the commissioners as in other cases, and at the rates prescribed thereon."

2. This act shall be in force from its passage. *Commencement.*

CHAP. 81.—An ACT amending and re-enacting the fourth section of the Ordinance passed June 21st, 1861.

Passed February 5, 1863.

1. Be it enacted by the General Assembly of Virginia, That the fourth section of the ordinance passed June 21st, 1861, be amended and re-enacted so as to read as follows: *The fourth section amended and re-enacted.*

"§4. That whenever the governor shall deem it expedient and for the public good, that the offices of the auditor and treasurer should be kept in the city of Alexandria or in any other place in the commonwealth outside of the city of Wheeling, he may issue a proclamation establishing the said offices of auditor and treasurer at Alexandria or such other place, as in his judgment he may deem best, and the executive is hereby authorized to convene the legislature at such place within the state of Virginia, as he may select, for the seat of government, under this act.

Commencement. 2. This act shall be in force from and after its passage.

CHAP. 82.—An ACT authorizing the revival of certain suits depending in the courts of the Commonwealth.

Passed February 5, 1863.

Suits pending in the courts of the commonwealth not to abate or be dismissed. 1. Be it enacted by the General Assembly, That all or any suits depending in any court of the commonwealth in the name of the board of public works, prior to the 9th day of August, 1861, shall not abate or be dismissed for want of authority in the said courts to prosecute them by reason of any change in the officer discharging the duties of said board, but may be revived (if necessary) in the name of the governor, auditor and treasurer of the commonwealth, acting as said board and discharging its duties as provided for by the ordinance of the convention of August 9th, 1861, anything in the act of the general assembly passed July 16th, 1861, to the contrary notwithstanding.

Commencement. 2. This act shall be in force from its passage.

CHAP. 83.—An ACT to authorize the Auditor of Public Accounts to appoint Commissioners of the Revenue in certain cases.

Passed February 5, 1863.

When the Auditor is requested to appoint Commissioners of the Revenue. 1. Be it enacted by the General Assembly of Virginia, That the auditor of public accounts is hereby authorized and required in counties and towns of this commonwealth, where the commissioner's books of said counties and towns cannot be found, and where commissioners have not been elected under the re-organized government of Virginia, to appoint commissioners of the revenue to assess the taxes due the commonwealth for the year 1862 and 1863, and forward the books for that purpose to said commissioners.

ommencement. 2. This act shall be in force from its passage.

CHAP. 84.—AN ACT amending and re-enacting section thirteenth of an act passed July 26, 1861, entitled an act to provide for the public health.

Passed February 5, 1863.

1. Be it enacted by the General Assembly, That section thirteen of an act passed July 26, 1861, entitled an act to provide for the public health, be amended and re-enacted so as to read as follows: *Section thirteen amended and re-enacted.*

"§13. The sum of five hundred dollars is hereby appropriated for the payment of such agent. The same, or so much thereof, as may be required, shall be paid semi-annually on the order of the governor, when he shall be satisfied that the agent has faithfully complied with his contract and duty, as agent, to the time of such payment."

2. This act shall be in force from its passage. *Commencement.*

CHAP. 85.—An ACT repealing an Act passed February 15th, 1862, entitled "An Act to provide for the payment of costs in prosecutions for misdemeanors, &c."

Passed February 5, 1863.

1. Be it enacted by the General Assembly of Virginia, That an act passed February 15th, 1862, entitled "an act to provide for the payment of costs in prosecutions for misdemeanors, &c.," be and the same is hereby repealed. *Act passed Feb. 15th, 1862, repealed.*

2. This act shall be in force from its passage. *Commencement.*

CHAP. 86.—An ACT to amend and re-enact an Act entitled "An Act to incorporate the Bank of Guyandotte," passed March 2d, 1854.

Passed February 5, 1863.

1. Be it enacted by the General Assembly, That sections first, second, third and eighth of an act entitled "an act to incorporate the Bank of Guyandotte, in the county of Cabell," passed March 2d, 1854, be amended and re-enacted so as to read as follows: *Sections first, second, third and eighth of an Act to incorporate the Bank of Guyandotte amended an re-enacted.*

"§1. It shall be lawful to establish a bank in the town of Guyandotte, in the county of Cabell, the capital stock of which shall be not less than one hundred thousand dollars nor more than three hundred thousand dollars, to be raised by subscription of shares of one hundred dollars each; books of subscription for the stock aforesaid to be opened on the second Monday of March, 1863, and remain open until one hundred thousand dollars is subscribed in the town of Guyandotte under the superintendence of John Laidley, Sr., Thomas J. Hayslip and James H. Poage, or any two of them, who shall have power, and their rights, powers and duties in relation to said bank shall be in all respects as far as may be applicable, such as are prescribed by the Code of Virginia. The commissioners shall be, and they are hereby authorized to receive subscriptions partly in money and partly in the stocks of the United States, the medium of payment to be expressed at the time of making such subscription, and the stock transferred to the bank and the money paid over as soon as the president and directors shall be elected.

"§2. The said bank shall be called "The Bank of Guyandotte," but the name may be changed to "The Bank of West Virginia" if the stockholders or directors shall so elect, and by said name and style the stockholders thereof and their successors shall be a body politic and corporate, with all the rights, powers and privileges conferred upon banks of the state by chapters fifty-seven and fifty-eight of the Code of Virginia, and shall moreover be subject to all the rules, regulations and restrictions imposed by the said chapters fifty-seven and fifty-eight, except the seventh section of said chapter fifty-eight, so far as said chapters are consistent with this act, provided that the stockholders shall appoint and elect directors.

"§3. Whenever the said bank shall legally transfer to deposit with the treasurer of the state, in trust for, and for the purposes of the said bank, certificates of the public debt of the United States, bearing six per centum interest, to the amount of fifty thousand dollars, the said bank shall be authorized to deliver notes of any denomination it may elect, not less than five dollars, to the treasurer in the usual form of bank notes intended for circulation, to the full amount of the stock so deposited, upon the face of which shall be written or printed the words "Secured by pledge of United States securities," and each bank note shall be countersigned by the treasurer and numbered and registered in proper books to be provided and kept for the purpose in the office of said treasurer; and such notes so countersigned shall be re-delivered to the officers of said bank, and the said bank so receiving the same may thereupon issue its notes aforesaid to the full amount of the stock so deposited, and from time to time upon further deposits of such certificates of debt of the United States by said bank, in sums not less than five thousand dollars; the said bank may in like manner issue notes countersigned as aforesaid to the full amount so deposited—but such issues shall not exceed in the aggregate the capital herein provided.

"§8. Each and every stockholder in said bank shall be liable rateably out of his private estate for the circulation and express contract debts of said bank to the amount of stock held by him, upon a failure of said bank to redeem its notes or pay said debts. The total amount of paper circulation of the bank hereby incorporated shall never exceed five times the amount of coin in possession and actually the property of the bank. If the coin be reduced to less than one-fifth of its paper circulation the bank shall thereupon make no new loan or discount until its coin shall be to its paper circulation at least the proportion of one to five: provided, however, that this act shall not take effect so as to authorize the said bank to make loans or discounts, or transact any other banking business until the minimum amount of *the capital hereby authorized shall be deposited in United States stock with the treasurer of this commonwealth, as is provided by the fourth section of this act. The costs to the state arising from the provisions of this act shall be paid by the said bank."

2. This act shall take effect from its passage. Commencement.

JOINT RESOLUTIONS.

No. 1.—Joint Resolution enquiring into the manner in which the duties of the Public Printer have been discharged.

Passed December 8, 1862.

Resolved, That a joint committee of eight, consisting of five from the house and three from the senate be appointed by the speaker and president of the same, to inquire into the manner in which the duties of public printer have been discharged, whether he has done all the public printing, and if so, how much and in what manner, whether any printing has been done for the state by any other person, and if so, at what price, in what manner and by whom authorized, and to report to this house such other matters concerning the same as they may deem proper, and that said committee have power to send for and have before them persons, books and papers to assist them in the said inquiry.

No. 2.—Joint Resolution requesting the House of Representatives of the United States to take up and pass without amendment, the bill for the admission of the State of West Virginia, passed by the United States Senate on the 10th of July last.

Passed December 9, 1862.

Resolved, That feeling the greatest anxiety and interest in the successful issue of the movement for a new state in West Virginia, we earnestly request the house of representatives of the United States to take up and pass, without alteration or amendments, the bill which passed the senate of the United States on the 10th of July last.

No. 3.—Joint Resolutions requesting the Hon. John S. Carlile to resign his seat in the Senate of the United States.

Passed December 12, 1862.

WHEREAS, The General Assembly of Virginia, by resolution adopted at the session of July, 1862, instructed the senators of this state in congress to sustain the federal government in its efforts to maintain the supremacy of the laws and preserve the integrity of the Union, and by a legislative act of the 13th of May, 1862, requested them to use their endeavors to obtain the consent of congress to the admission of West Virginia into the Union; and whereas, the Hon. John S. Carlile having failed not only to sustain the legitimate efforts of the federal government to suppress the insurrection, but having opposed by his votes in the senate, and public speeches in and out of the senate, measures absolutely necessary to the preservation of the Union and the enforcement of the laws, and having also by his speeches and votes in the senate opposed the bill for the admission of West Virginia into the Union; therefore,

Resolved, By the General Assembly, That inasmuch as he has neither regarded the instructions aforesaid, nor the known will of the loyal people of the state, he is hereby respectfully requested to resign his seat.

Resolved, That the governor be requested to forward copies of these resolutions to our senators and representatives in congress, with a request that the same be laid before congress.

No. 4.—Joint Resolution appointing a joint committee to inquire into the Permit System.

Passed December 12, 1862.

Resolved, That a joint committee to consist of three members from the house and two from the senate, be appointed to inquire into the "permit" system now enforced by the agents of the treasury department, with a view to relieve, if possible, the citizens of this state from the inconvenience and injury imposed upon them under its present operations.

No. 5.—Joint Resolution directing the Auditor to issue to the heirs generally of Walter Brooke, a land warrant for five thousand acres.

Passed January 10, 1863.

WHEREAS, It appears to the general assembly that the heirs of Commodore Walter Brooke in the war of the revolution, are entitled to five thousand acres of additional land bounty from the State of Virginia, for the service of their ancestor, the said Walter Brooke, in the war of the revolution; and whereas, by reason of the existing rebellion the warrant for the said additional amount of land bounty cannot be had from the land office at Richmond, Therefore

Resolved, by the General Assembly, That Samuel Crane, the auditor of this commonwealth, be, and he is hereby directed to issue to the heirs generally of the said Walter Brooke, a land warrant for the balance of bounty due to them, to-wit: five thousand acres, that amount being acknowledged by the register of the land office at Richmond, to be so due.

JOINT RESOLUTIONS.

No. 6.—Joint Resolution of Condolence.

Passed January 10, 1863.

WHEREAS, It has been made known to the General Assembly of Virginia, that on Tuesday the 6th day of January, 1863, Mrs. Tarr, wife of Campbell Tarr, Esq., treasurer of the state of Virginia, departed this life.

Resolved, That in this bereavement of our worthy treasurer the general assembly tenders to him its deepest regrets and sincere sympathy at the dispensation.

No. 7.—Joint resolution of thanks to Dr. Hills, Superintendent of the Insane Asylum at Columbus, Ohio, for his kind and humane treatment to the insane of this State.

Passed January 10, 1863.

Resolved, by the Senate and House of Delegates of Virginia, That the thanks of the state of Virginia are justly due and are hereby tendered to Dr. Hills, superintendent of the asylum at Columbus, Ohio, for the kind and humane treatment extended by him to the unfortunate insane of this state, who, because of the present rebellion, could not be received and treated in the lunatic asylums of this commonwealth.

Resolved, That the governor be requested to transmit a copy of these resolutions to Dr. Hills.

No. 8.—Joint Resolution to elect a Public Printer.

Passed January 19, 1863.

Resolved, That this house will, with the concurrence of the senate, proceed to the election of a public printer at eleven o'clock, a. m., on Wednesday next.

No. 9.—Joint Resolution to elect a United States Senator.

Passed January 21, 1863.

Resolved, By the General Assembly of Virginia, that both houses by a joint vote proceed on Friday the 23d inst., at 12 o'clock, m., to elect a United States senator.

No. 10.—Joint Resolution to employ a Janitor for the Public Buildings.

Passed January 29, 1863.

Resolved, That the governor be authorized to employ a janitor for the public buildings.

JOINT RESOLUTIONS.

No. 11.—Joint Resolution releasing the late Public Printer from the payment of Four Hundred and Ten Dollars, upon conditions.

Passed February 4, 1863.

WHEREAS, by the report of the committee on public printing, it appears that A. S. Trowbridge, as public printer, is indebted to the state in the amount of four hundred and ten dollars, being for over charges on work done by him as public printer; and whereas, said Trowbridge has printed a number of reams of commissioner's books which the auditor refused to receive or pay for; and whereas, public printing to which the said Trowbridge was entitled by law, was withheld from him by an officer or officers of the government, thus depriving him of the revenue or profits therefrom, Therefore be it

Resolved, The senate concurring, that the auditor, be, and is hereby authorized and required to receive from the said A. S. Trowbridge the commissioner's books herein referred to, and that upon delivery of said books to the auditor, the said Trowbridge is hereby discharged of his indebtedness to the state in the amount of four hundred and ten dollars aforesaid: provided, however, that nothing in the foregoing preamble and resolution, shall be so construed as a reflection upon the auditor of public accounts for withholding printing from A. S. Trowbridge, late public printer.

No. 12. Joint Resolution authorizing the Governor to procure and present to the Seventh Regiment, Virginia Volunteer Infantry, a suitable flag.

Passed February 4, 1863.

Resolved, The senate concurring, that the Governor be authorized and requested to procure and present to the 7th Regiment Virginia Volunteer Infantry a suitable flag, with the following inscription: "Seventh (Union) Virginia Volunteers, Antietam, September 17th, 1862," on one side, and on the other side "Fredericksburg, Dec. 13th, 1862."

No. 13.—Joint Resolution appropriating Fifty Dollars to the Clerk of the House, in addition to his present compensation.

Passed February 4, 1863.

Resolved, by the General Assembly, That the sum of fifty dollars be appropriated to the clerk of the house of delegates, in addition to his present compensation, to be paid out of the appropriation for expenses of the general assembly.

JOINT RESOLUTIONS. 83

No. 14.—Joint Resolution directing the Auditor of Public Accounts to settle with Samuel W. Wilson, Sheriff of Hancock County.

Passed February 5, 1863.

Resolved, by the General Assembly, That the auditor of public accounts be directed to settle with Samuel W. Wilson, sheriff of Hancock county, and allow him his delinquent list of land, property, capitation and license tax for 1860, if found by the auditor to be correct, upon the condition that the said sheriff pay into the treasury any sums upon settlement found due the state.

No. 15.—Joint Resolutions in reference to retaliation and indemnity.

Passed February 5, 1863.

WHEREAS, It is represented to this General Assembly, that the rebels in Virginia have arrested and now have confined in prisons, many loyal citizens, civilians and non-combatants, including men, women and children, on the pretence of their disloyalty to the pretended southern confederacy; and whereas, the said rebels have robbed many of our loyal citizens of large amounts of money and property; therefore, be it

Resolved, By the general assembly of Virginia, that the president of the United States be, and he is hereby respectfully requested to order military officers of the general government in this state to retaliate by arresting such a number of known adherents to, or avowed sympathizers with, the said pretended confederacy, as in his opinion may be expedient, to be held in close confinement as hostages, and be subject in all respects, as nearly as may be, to the same treatment which is imposed upon loyal citizens by the authority of the said pretended confederacy; and to adopt such other and further measures as shall be necessary to effect the release of such loyal persons as are now or may hereafter be so arrested and confined; and that the president be further requested to require the military authorities, to institute such measures as will compel the rebels and those aiding and assisting them in any degree in the arrest and robbery of our loyal citizens, to fully indemnify those loyal citizens for all losses by said robberies.

Be it further resolved, That we fully and heartily endorse the course pursued by General Milroy for the protection and indemnity of the loyal ciitzens of Western Virginia, and we respectfully ask the general government to sustain him in his action looking to the indemnity of the loyal citizens aforesaid, and that the government be requested to instruct the military in this commonwealth to pursue a similar course, as we believe that it is the most efficient means of protecting the property of our loyal citizens.

Resolved further, That the governor be, and he is hereby requested to communicate the foregoing preamble and resolutions to the president of the United States, together with a list of the names and condition, so far as may be known to him, of the persons so held in confinement, or robbed as aforesaid, with such other information pertinent to the subject as he may deem expedient.

No. 16.—Joint Resolution requesting the President of the United States and Secretary of War to direct the transfer of the Seventh (Union) Regiment Virginia Volunteer Infantry to the Western Virginia service.

Passed Februrry 5, 1863.

WHEREAS, it has been represented to the General Assembly of Virginia, That the seventh (Union) regiment Virginia volunteer infantry has been in the service in eastern Virginia, in the army of the Potomac, during the greater portion of the time since they were mustered into the service of the United States, during which time they have done much hard service; and that they took a very active part in the battles of Antietam and Fredericksburg, Va., during which their losses were very heavy; and that by sickness and death during their long campaign on the peninsula, their ranks have greatly reduced, Therefore be it

Resolved, by the General Assembly of Virginia, That the president of the United States and the secretary of war, be, and they are hereby requested to direct the transfer of said regiment to the Western Virginia service.

SEPARATE ELECTION PRECINCTS.

Accomack—Court-house; Chingoteague; New Church; Corbin and Fletcher's; Mapp's; Guilford; Newstown; Onancock; Pungoteage.

Albemarle—Court-house; Lindsay's Turnout; Everettsville; Stony Point; Earleysville; Blackwell's; Free Union; Whitehall; Woodville; Batesville; Hillsborough; Crossroads; Covesville; Porter's; Warren; Wingfield's; Milton; Scottsville; Monticello House; Howardsville.

Alexandria—Five districts—identical with magisterial districts.

Alleghany Court house; Robert Skeen's Hotel; John O. Taylor's; George Stull's; Clifton Forge; Jabez Johnston's; Griffith's Mill; Fork Run.

Amelia—At the same place as magisterial elections.

Amherst—New Glasgow; New Hope; Oronoco; Chestnut Grove; Folly; Temperance; Pedlar Mills; Elon; Court-house; Buffalo Springs.

Appomattox—Court-house; Union Academy; Wesley Chapel; Hamner's; Spout Spring; Oakville.

Augusta—Court-house; Waynesborough; Middlebrook; Spring Hill; Mt. Meridian; Greensville; District No. 2, Staunton; Mt. Sidney; Stuart's Draft; Fishersville; Churchville; New Hope; Craigsville; Deerfield; Mt. Solon; Swoop's Mill; Midway; Newport.

Barbour—Court-house; Burner's; Nutter's; Bartlett's; Mitchell's; Yeager's; Glady Creek; Holtsberry's; Coal Precinct.

Bath—Court-house; Cedar Creek; Hamilton's; Cleek's Mills; Williamsville; Milton; Green Valley.

Berkeley—Court-house; Billingre's Hotel; Mill Creek; Hedgesville; Falling Waters; Robinson's Mill; Gerrardstown; Oak Grove; Glen Spring; Crossroads.

Boone—Court-house, Adkins' on Mud river, Adkins' on Big Coal, Lawrence's, Curtiss', Daniel Laurel's, Thompson's Mill, Miller's.

Botetourt—Court-house, Mountain Union, Carver's, Buchanan, Rocky Point Mills, Jackson, Junction Store, Dibrell's Spring, Amsterdam.

Braxton—Court-house, Triplett's, Rilney's, Cool's, John Crite's former residence, Christian Moda's former residence, Haymond's Mill, Cunningham's, Saulsberry, Stenestreet, Jacob P. Conrad's.

Brooke—At same places as magisterial elections, Goodwill School house.

Brunswick—Court-house, Benton precinct, Trotty's Store, Oak Grove, Lucy's Store, Smoky Ordinary, Nicholson's precinct.

Buckingham—Court-house, Stanton's shop, New Store, Wright's, Curdsville, Allen's.

Cabell—Court-house, Guyandotte, Laidley's Store, Spurlock's, Doolittle's Mill, Barret's Precinct, McComas', Falls of Guyandotte, Kilgore's Precinct, Peter Buffington's.

Campbell—Places the same as for magisterial elections.

Caroline—Court-house, Reedy Church, Oakley's, Needwood, Sparta, Pitts', Port Royal, Sycamore, Golansville, Madison's.

Carroll—Court-house, Polly Quesenberry's, Thomas Quesenberry's, Laurel Fork, Kinney's, Easter's, Newman's, Sulphur Springs, Richard Haynes', Nathaniel Haynes'.

Charles City—Court-house, Delarue's, Ladd's, Waddell's, Apperson's, Vaiden's.

Charlotte—Court-house, Keysville, Smith's Tavern, Clement's, Wyliesburg, Roby's Shop, Hawrey's Store, Matthews & Smith's Store.

Chesterfield—Court-house, Britton's Shop, Shell's Tavern, Manchester, Robinson's Store, Clover Hill.

Clarke—Court-house, Russell's Tavern, White Post, Millwood, Royston's Tavern, Collier's Toll-gate.

Craig—Court-house, Carper's Tavern, Walker's Store, Scott's Tavern, Martin Huffman's George Sarver's.

Culpeper—Court-house, Rixyville, Colvin's, Stevensburg, Pottsville, Gathright's, Wellsborough, Griffinsburg.

Cumberland—Court-house, Tavern Precinct, Oak Forest, Irwin's.

Dinwiddie—Court-house, Billups', Goodwynsville, Williams' Shop, Darvill's, Williams', Sutherland's.

Doddridge—Court-house, Allen's, Bond's, Key's, Davis'.

Elizabeth City—Court-house, Liveley's Ordinary, Fox Hill.

Essex—Court-house, Occupacion, Lloyd's, Miller's, Bestland, Centre Cross.

Fairfax—Court-house, Crossroads, Arundel's, Sangster, Ross', Bowden's

SEPARATE ELECTION PRECINCTS. 87

(Springvale), Anandale, West End, Accotink, Centreville, Falls Church, Fars, Bayless, Pulman's.

Fauquier—Court-house, Plains, Salem, White Ridge, Farrowsville, Orleans, Liberty, Morrisville, Paris, New Baltimore, Rectortown, Weaversville, Upperville.

Fayette—Court-house, Blake's, Gauley Bridge, Fleshman's, Lewis', Keeney's, Terry's, Coleman's.

Fluvanna—Court-house, Howard's Store, Columbia, Morris' Store, Kent's Store, Haden's Store, Bashan and Snead's, Bledsoe's, Union Grove.

Franklin—Court-house, Allen's, Union Hall, Booth's Store, McVey's Tanyard, Helm's. Dickerson's, Kinsey's, Richland Grove, Bush's Store, Sydnorsville, Snow Creek, Aldridge's Store.

Frederick—Court-house, Engine-house, Gwinn's Tavern, Hoover's Tavern, Newtown, Middlotown, Russell's, Anderson's, Brucetown, Swheir's, Cole's School-house, Pughtown.

Giles—At the same places as magisterial elections, Howe's Hotel.

Gilmer—Court-house, Jerkland, Burke's Widow Stumps, De Kalb's, Peregrine Hays', Knotts', Hewett's, Troy.

Goochland—Court-house, Little Store, Perkinsville, Smith's Shop, Mill's, Holland's, Poor's, Jennings'.

Gloucester—Places the same as for magisterial elections.

Greenbrier—Court-house, Blue Sulphur Springs, Lick Creek, Anthony's Creek, Spring Creek, Southside, Lewisburg, White Sulphur, Miller's; Irish Corner, Williamsburg, Frankfort.

Greene—Court-house, Ruckersville, Terrill Shiflett's, McMullansville.

Greensville—Court-house, Ryland's Depot, Blunt's Mill, Poplar Mount.

Halifax—Court-house, Meadesville, Mount Carmel, Halifax Springs, High Hill, Hudson's, Garret's Store, Whiteville, Republican Grove, Brooklyn.

Hampshire—Court-house, John Liller's, Miers', Burlington, Taylor's, Doyles', Thompson's, Lupton's, Kisner's, Lovett's, Mrs. Offutt's, Stump's, Fority, Sherrard's School-house, Hash's, Blair's, Arnold's, Piedmont.

Hancock—Court-house, Holliday's Cove, New Manchester, Aton's School-house.

Hanover—Court-house, Hughes', Jones' Crossroads, Negrofoot, Dentonsville, Cold Harbor, Ashland.

SEPARATE ELECTION PRECINCTS.

Harrison—Court-house, Shinnston, Union Meeting-house, West Milford, Lumberport, Bridgeport, Davis', Lynch's, Sardis, Swisher's Mills, Rockford School-house.

Henrico—Court-house, Kidd's, Sweeney's, Alley's, Lovingsteine's, Dickman's, Hughes', Walkerton, Hungary.

Henry—Court-house, Rough and Ready, Irisburg, Oak Level, Leatherwood, Ridgeway, Horse Pasture.

Highland—Monterey, Ruckmansville, Wiley's, Crab Bottom, Doe Hill, McDowell, Pullin's School-house, Gwin's.

Jackson—Ripley, Click's, Jones', Range's, California, Depue's, Three forks of Reedy, Trumansville, Ravenswood, School-house near Staat's, Murrayville, Moor's Mill, McGrew's Mill, Reed's (in place of Sandyville.)

James City—Court-house, Burnt Ordinary, York river.

Jefferson—Eight districts—Places the same as for magisterial elections.

Kanawha—Court-house, Fleetwood's, Richard's, Bradley Low's, Atkinson's Mill, Altz's, Couts' Mouth, Dog Creek, Givens', Malden, Fork Coal, Harper's, Gatewood's, Mouth Sandy, Brooks' Store.

King George—Court-house, Hampstead, Clifton, Shiloh.

King & Queen—Court-house, Clark's Store, Stevensville, Newtown, Centreville.

King William—Court-house, Plain Dealing, Aylett's, Lanesville.

Lancaster—Court-house, Litwalton, Kilmanock, White Stone.

Lewis—Court-house, McLaughlin's Store, Jane Lew, Freeman's Creek, Skin Creek, Hall's Store, Leading Creek, Collins' Settlement.

Logan—Same places as for magisterial elections.

Loudoun—Court-house, Waterford, Lovetsville, Hillsborough, Waters', Purcell's Store, Snickersville, Union, Middleburg, Mt. Gilead, Gum Spring, Whaley's, Goresville.

Louisa—Court-house, Free Union, Hopkins' Mill, Trevilian's, Bell's Crossroads, Walton's Tavern, Terrill's Store, Parrish's Store, Frederickshall, Bumpass' Turnout, Thompson's Crossroads, Isabell's Store, Hope's Tavern, Gentry's Store, Cosby's Tavern.

Lunenburg—Court-house, Brown's store, Pleasant Grove, Knight and Oliver's Mill, Lochlomond, Bagley's Store, Jordon's Store.

Madison—Court-house, Stony Hill, Criglersville, Huffman's Mill, Graves' Mill, Rapidan Meeting-house, Fleshman's Shop, Locust Dale.

SEPARATE ELECTION PRECINCTS. 89

Marion—Places the same as those for magisterial elections, and at Glover's Gap.

Marshall—Court-house, Pleasant Hill, Jones' Hotel, Bleak's Schoolhouse, Parsons' Precinct, Mouth of Fish Creek, Sand Hill, Crossroads, Smart's School-house, Burley's, Terrill's School-house, Big Run, Fair View, Linn Camp.

Mason—Court-house, Berriage Precinct, Love Precinct, Barnett Precinct, West Columbia, Neaso Precinct, Eighteen Mile Precinct, Grigg's, Sixteen Mile Precinct, Thirteen Mile Precinct.

Matthews—Same places as for magisterial elections.

Mecklenburg—Court-house, Jones', Edmundson's Clarkesville, Reeke's, Overby's, Wright's, Harwell's, Christiansville, Gillespie's.

Middlesex—Jamaica, Saludo, Sandy Bottom.

Monongalia—Court-house, Guseman's, Jones', Osburn's, Ross', Lofter's, Cassville, Cristiman's, Laurel Point, Cox's, Moore's River, Tenant's, Dowall's, Warren, Arnett's

Monroe—Court-house, Dickson's, Miller's Store, Rollinsburg, Mrs. Peck's, Red Sulphur, Hayne's, Centreville.

Montgomery—Court-house, Guerrant's, Peterman's, Price's, Forks, Keister's, Crumpacker's, Layfayette, Kent and McConkey's, Rough and Ready, Lovely Mount.

Morgan—Court-house, Lowe's, Baker's, Bazzoc Shockey's, Swann's, Miller's.

Nansemond—Court-house, Hargrove's Tavern, Harrison's Shop, Hollyneck, Chuckatuck, Somerton, Darden's Store, Cypress Chapel.

Nelson—Fortune's, New Market, Faber's Mill, Greenfield, Massie's Mill, Roberts'.

New Kent—Court-house, Barhamsville, Chandler's Store, Ratcliff's Tavern.

Nicholas—Court-house, Taylor's, Brown's, Neil's, Dunbar's, Nutter's, Sawyer's, Pierson's.

Norfolk City—Four Wards.

Norfolk County—Court-house, Glebe School-house, Sycamore's, Deep Creek, School-house District No. 2, School-house in Providence, Pleasant Grove School-house, Butts' Road School-house.

Northampton—Court-house, Bay View, Franktown, Johnsontown, Capeville.

SEPARATE ELECTION PRECINCTS.

Northumberland—Court-house, Lottsburg, Burgess' Store, Wicomico.

Nottoway—Court-house, Jennings' Ordinary, Wilson and Jones', Blackfare.

Ohio—M'Connell's, West Liberty, Atkinson's, Triadelphia, 1st Ward Hose House, Court House, 4th Ward Hose House, 5th Ward School House.

Orange—Court-house, Barboursville, Thomas Smith's, Thomas Rhoade's, Locust Grove.

Page—Court-house, Honeyville, Oakham, George Price's Mill, Springfield, Mohler's Mill, Rileysville, Prunty's Mill.

Patrick—Court-house, Robertson's, Aldridge's and Lee's, Penn's Store, Carter's Store, Hancock's, Elamsville, Slusher's, Connor's, Shilor's, Gates', Mankin's.

Pendleton—Franklin, Harper's, Kiser's, Vint's, Cowyer's Mill, Mallow's, Seneca, Circleville.

Petersburg—Centre Ward, East Ward, South Ward, West Ward.

Pittsylvania—Court-house, Danville, Spring Garden, Whitmell, Cascade, Smith's, Beaver's, Raceville, Rorer's, Strail's Store, White's, Laurel Grove, Chalk Level, Mooman's.

Pleasants—Court-house, Spring Run, Sugar Creek, Gorrel's, Hale's Mill.

Pocahontas—Four districts—Places of election the same as for magistrates.

Powhattan—Court-house, Clark's Mill, Macon, Sublett's.

Preston—Brandonville, Miller's, Burnel's, Feather's, Summit Schoolhouse, Germany, Graham's, Gordon's, Kingwood, Martin's, Independence, Evansville, Brown's, Funk's.

Princess Anne—Court-house, Kempsville, London Bridge, Capp's Shop, Creed's Bridge, Blackwater.

Prince Edward—Court-house, Marble Hill, Spring Creek, Prospect, Farmville, Sandy River.

Price George—Court-house, City Point, Lilley's School-house, Tuttle's Precinct, Harrison's Store, Templeton.

Prince William—Dumfries, Cole's, Occoquan, Reeve's, Brentsville, Kinchelon's, Haymarket, Ludley.

Pulaski—Court-house, Brown's, Galbreath's, Ruper's, Thorn Spring Camp.

Putnam—Court-house, Bailey's, Pocatalico, Alexander's, Red House, Jones', Hurricane Bridge, Wheeler's, Buffalo, Eighteen Mile Precinct.

SEPARATE ELECTION PRECINCTS. 91

Raleigh—Same places as magisterial elections.

Randolph—Court-house, Pennington's, Minear's, Taylor's, Kemp's, Lee.

Rappahannock—Washington, Sperryville, Yates', Amissville, Catharine Deatheridge.

Richmond City—Jefferson Ward, Madison Ward, Monroe Ward.

Richmond County—Court-house, Stony Hill, Tavern-house, Farnham Church, Lyell's Store.

Ritchie—Harrisville, Skelton's, Leedan's, Ireland's, Deems', Rawson's, Tebbs', Murphy's.

Roanoke—Court-house, Big Lick, Cave Spring, Barnett's.

Rockbridge—Court-house, Brownsburg, Fairfield, Natural Bridge, Collierstown, Keer's Creek, Trevey's, Hamilton's School-house, Paxton's School-house, Wilson's Shop, Broad Creek, Goshen.

Rockingham—Harrisonburg, Keezletown, McGaheysville, Conrad's Store, Spartapolis, Henton's Mills, Gordon's Store, Bowman's Mill, Timberville, Menonite School-house, Bridgewater, Ottobine, Wittig's Store, Sprinkle's Store, Taliaferro's Store, Port Republic, Mount Crawford, Samuel Coot's.

Russell—Court-house, Grizle's, Pound, Holly Creek, Guest's Mountain, Castlewood's Fugate's, Hanson's, Aston's Store, Cook's Mills, Dorton's, Baylor's Store, Gibson's, Hendrick's Store.

Scott—Court-house, Wineger's, Hart's, Smith's, Puilleng's, Nickelsville, Alleys, Osborne's Ford, Stony Creek, Peters', Rye Cove, Carter's, Neil's, Roller's.

Shenandoah—Court-house, Strasburg, Crossroads Meeting-house, Conner's Church, Town Hall, Keller's School-house, Edinburg, Columbia Furnace, Mount Jackson, Crossroads School-house, New Market, Forrestville.

Smyth—Court-house, Broad Ford, Hays', Sanders', St. Clair's Bottom, Burton's Store, Ashlin's, Atkins'.

Spotsylvania—Court-house, Fredericksburg, Mount Pleasant, Andrew's, Chancellor's.

Stafford—Court-house, White Oak, Master's, Tackett's Mill, Falmouth, Coakleys, Harwood's, Acquia.

Southampton—Court-house, Drewrysville, Crosskeys, Joyner's, Murfee's, Black Creek Church, Berlin, Faison's Store.

Surry—Four districts—At the same places as for election of magistrates.

Sussex—Court-house, Comann's Mill, Henry, Stony Creek, Newville, Owen's Store.

SEPARATE ELECTION PRECINCTS.

Taylor—Court-house, Mahaney, Grey's, Claysville, Knottsville, Haymond's, Fetterman, Grafton.

Tazewell—Court-house, Repass, Tiffany's, Mouth of Slate, Gibson's, Crabtree's, Litzeville, Liberty Hill, Tugg.

Tyler—Court-house, Centreville, David John's, Hammond's, Underwood's, Dancer's, Sistersville, Pleasant Mills.

Upshur—Court-house, Reedy Mills, Simpson's Mill, Posty, Marples, Marshall's, Chesney's.

Warren—Court-house, Boyd's Mill, Bentonville, Leary's School-house, Cedarville, Howellsville.

Warwick—Three precincts—The same as for election of magistrates.

Washington—Court-house, Clark's, Davis', Waterman's, Merchant's, Gobble's, Mills', Worley's, Williams', Morrell's, Fullen's School-house, Clark's, Kelly's School-house, Delusko Mills, Ons', Miller's, Good Hope, Green Spring.

Wayne—William Crums. (No other returned.)

Westmoreland—Court-house, Hague, Warrensville, Oak Grove.

Wetzel—Court-house, Forks of Proctor, Knob Fork, Church's, Cohorn's, Ice's, Willey's School-house.

Williamsburg—Court-house.

Wirt—Court-house, Foster's, Petty's.

Wood—Precincts at the same place as election for migistrates.

Wyoming—Court-house, Gad's, Rhinehart's, McKinney's, Bailey's, Lester's.

Wythe—Eight districts—Precincts at same places as for election of magistrates.

York—Three districts—Precincts at the same places as for election of magistrates.

A LIST OF COMMISSIONERS

In other States, &c., appointed by the Executive of Virginia during the years 1858 and 1859, with the Residence and Date of Appointment of each Commissioner—also the Date when Evidence of his Qualification was filed.

[The term of office of commissioner is two years.]

States, &c.	Names of Commissioners.	Residence.	Date of Appointment.	When evidence of Qualification filed.
Alabama,	Wiley T. Hawkins	Florence	Feb. 26, 1858	Mar. 24, 1858
"	Asher Clarkson	Sumpter co.	May 16, 1859	May 28, 1859
"	H. B. Holcombe	Mobile	July 19 "	Sept. 26 "
Arkansas,	Moses H. Eastman	Little Rock	Aug. 29 "	Not filed.
"	James H. Gray	Jackson co.	Sept. 12 "	"
California,	Sam'l Hermann, jr.	San Francisco	Jan. 26, 1858	"
"	L. W. Sloat	do	Feb. 18 "	"
"	A. K. Grin	Sacramento city	Mar. 17 "	May 15, 1858
"	F. J. Thibault	San Francisco	Aug. 10 "	Dec. 14 "
"	Wm. B. Latham, jr.	Marysville, Yuba county	Sept. 14 "	Not filed.
"	Robert C. Page	San Francisco	April 27, 1859	Sept. 14, 1859
"	William G. English	Sacramento	May 16 "	Aug. 12 "
"	C. J. Brenham	San Francisco	July 13 "	Sept. 12 "
"	George Fisher	do	Aug. 12 "	Dec. 2 "
"	John Banning	do	Nov. 29 "	Not filed.
Connecticut,	Hubbard Arnold	New Haven	Jan. 30, 1858	"
"	Edward Goodman	Hartford	Feb. 5 "	Feb. 16, 1858
"	Charles J. Hoadley	do	April 17 "	May 5 "
"	Charles Whittlesey	do	July 15, 1859	July 21, 1859
Delaware,	William B. Wiggins	Wilmington	July 10, 1858	Sept. 21, 1858
Dis. Columbia,	Anthony Hyde	Georgetown	Feb. 5 "	Feb. 23 "
"	Charles De Selding	Washington	Mar. 27 "	Mar. 31 "
"	S. S. Williams	do	July 17 "	Not filed.
"	Nicholas Callan	do	July 30 "	Aug. 2, 1858
"	John McKenney	do	Sept. 4 "	Oct. 7 "
"	J. S. Hollingshead	do	Sept. 4 "	Dec. 11 "
"	William S. Clary	do	Sept. 13 "	Not filed.
"	Frederick Callan	do	Oct. 4 "	"
"	Robert White	Georgetown	Feb. 24, 1859	Mar. 4, 1859
"	A. S. Meyer	Washington	April 7 "	April 15 "
Florida,	Aristides Doggett	Jacksonville	Mar. 20, 1858	Not filed.
"	Oscar Hart	do	May 24 "	"
"	M. P. de Rioboo	Pensacola	Dec. 2 "	"
Georgia,	A. H. H. Dawson	Savannah	Feb. 18 "	"
"	Frank H. Miller	Augusta	June 21 "	July 12, 1858
Illinois,	Philip A. Hoyne	Chicago	April 6 "	April 17 "
"	John H. Magill	do	Aug. 9 "	Not filed.
"	Gerhard Foreman	do	Aug. 13 "	Sept. 18, 1858
"	O. R. W. Lull	do	Sept. 21 "	Nov. 23 "
"	Samuel C. Smith	do	Dec. 7 "	Jan. 13, 1859
"	George H. Stone	Peoria	Mar. 28, 1859	June 10 "
"	George Wilmot	do	Sept. 28 "	Oct. 20 "
"	Nelson Thomasson	Chicago	Dec. 20 "	Not filed.
Indiana,	William Y. Wiley	Indianapolis	June 15 "	June 25, 1859
Iowa,	Samuel M. Rankin	Keokuk	July 29 "	Not filed.
Kansas,	E. F. Havens	Leavenworth city	May 24, 1858	"
Kentucky,	Daniel W. Lindsey	Frankfort	Feb. 15 "	"
"	John A. Monroe	do	Mar. 25 "	April 15, 1858

States, &c.	Names of Commissioners.	Residence.	Date of Appointment.	When evidence of Qualification filed.
Kentucky,	Joseph B. Kinkaid	Louisville	Aug. 25, 1858	Sept. 15, 1858
"	W. H. Cunningham	Henderson co.	Sept. 16 "	Sept. 16 "
"	John T. Dye	Maysville,	Dec. 3 "	Not filed.
"	Chas. L. Thompson	Louisville	June 15, 1859	"
Louisiana,	George L. Hill	New Orleans	Mar. 3, 1858	Mar. 19, 1858
"	Wm. Shannon	do	May 28 "	June 4 "
"	Arthur C. Waugh	do	July 8 "	Not filed.
"	Henry Pitts	Shreveport	Oct. 6 "	"
"	Adolph Mazureau	New Orleans	Jan. 20, 1859	"
"	Walter H. Peters	do	April 8 "	April 22, 1859
"	Charles W. Pope	Baton Rouge	June 20 "	Not filed.
"	De Witt C. Jones	Bayou Sara	Oct. 8 "	"
Maryland,	W. K. Falls	Baltimore city	Feb. 18, 1858	"
"	Jabez D. Pratt	do	Mar. 28 "	Mar. 17, 1858
"	A. H. Pennington	do	Mar. 31 "	Mar. 31 "
"	James B. Latimer	do	April 1 "	April 26 "
"	Joseph T. Atkinson	do	May 25 "	May 24 "
"	Dalyrmple Williams	do	May 14 "	May 26 "
"	John M. Torney	do	Sept. 1 "	Sept. 22, 1859
"	John H. Parkhill	do	Oct. 21 "	Oct. 27 "
"	John R. Kenley	do	Mar. 8, 1859	Mar. 11 "
"	F. Mearis,	do	Sept. 22 "	Not filed.
"	John R. D. Bedford	Baltimore co.	Oct. 15 "	"
"	E. R. Sprague	Baltimore city	Oct. 27 "	Oct. 31, 1859
Massachusetts,	J. R. Coolridge	Boston	Jan. 30, 1858	Mar. 5, 1858
"	George T. Angell	do	April 1 "	Mar. 31 "
"	Chas. B. F. Adams	do	April 15 "	April 21 "
"	Benj. H. Currier	do	May 6 "	May 6 "
"	J. H. Buckingham	do	June 21 "	Sept. 17, 1858, and resignation received Jan. 24, 1859
"	N. T. Leonard	Westfield	Jan. 18, 1859	Jan. 31 "
"	W. E. P. Smyth	Boston	Jan. 24 "	Not filed.
"	Elihu C. Baker	do	June 27 "	"
"	Abram G. Randall	Milbury, Worcester county	July 30 "	"
"	Benjamin Pond	Boston	Dec. 6 "	"
Michigan,	Wm. J. Waterman	Detroit	June 18, 1859	June 25, 1859
Minnesota,	Edward G. Odioine	St. Paul	Mar. 16, 1858	Dec. 16, 1858
"	Theodore Read	do	May 18 "	Not filed.
Missisippi,	B. W. Walthall	Holly Springs	Mar. 7, 1859	Mar. 22, 1859
Missouri,	Th. H. Teagarden	St. Louis	Feb. 4, 1858	Not filed.
"	Jas. E. Jenkins	do	Mar. 5 "	"
"	T. A. Russell	Kansas city, Jackson co.	Mar. 26 "	"
"	Jas. R. Goff	St. Louis	April 14 "	May 15, 1858
"	Edw'd W. Shands	do	May 11 "	June 12 "
"	Robert Stevens	do	May 28 "	June 21 "
"	H. S. Schuermann	do	Sept. 2 "	Sept. 21 "
"	James Hall	Kansas city	Oct. 8 "	Mar. 16, 1859
"	C. W. Bryan	Hannibal, Marion county	Feb. 7, 1959	Mar. 23, 1859
"	John A. Foster	Springfield, Greene co.	Mar. 9 "	Mar. 28 "
"	Joel G. Harper	St. Louis	Sept. 20 "	Oct. 1 "
"	Matthew R. Cullen	do	Oct. 24 "	Not filed.
"	Wm. H. Brand	Boonville	Nov. 23 "	Dec. 5, 1859
New Jersey,	James M. Cassady	Camden	Aug. 30, 1858	April 16 "
"	John J. Searing	Newark	Mar. 14, 1859	Mar. 19, 1859

COMMISSIONERS OF DEEDS. 95

States, &c.	Names of Commissioners.	Residence.	Date of Appointment.	When evidence of Qualification filed.
New Jersey,	William Burnett	Jersey city	Dec. 15, 1858	Not filed.
New York,	Michael L. Hiller	New York city	Jan. 16, 1858	Jan. 25, 1858
"	H. H. Woods	do	Jan. 30 "	Not filed.
"	G. S. Hutchinson	do	Feb. 15 "	Mar. 3, 1858
"	Calvin N. Northrop	New York city	Feb. 25, 1858	Aug. 10, 1858
"	Jos. C. Lawrence	do	Mar. 5 "	Mar. 31 "
"	Chas. J. Bushnell	do	April 1 "	Mar. 17 "
"	Wm. C. Ford	Brooklyn	April 15 "	April 6 "
"	Mosses B. Maclay	New York city	Mar. 31 "	Mar. 17 "
"	Augustin P. Mauge	do	Mar. 15 "	Mar. 20 "
"	Henry E. Marvin	do	Mar. 30 "	April 26 "
"	Daniel M. Porter	do	Mar. 31 "	Not filed.
"	Julius R. Pomeroy	Brooklyn	April 10 "	April 17, 1858
"	Rob't P. Neale	New York city	April 17 "	Not filed.
"	Benj. A. Hedgman	do	April 17 "	May 1, 1858
"	J. L. Marcellus	do	April 17 "	April 20 "
"	Wm. Brooke	do	April 19 "	Not filed.
"	Benj. A. Lavander	do	April 22 "	May 1, 1858
"	Zephaniah Platt	do	April 20 "	May 15 "
"	Wm. J. Sinclair	do	May 20 "	May 1 "
"	Amasa C. Moore	do	April 26 "	Dec. 6 "
"	Chas. H. Smith	do	May 1 "	Sep. 14 "
"	R. A. Watkinson	do	May 21 "	June 7 "
"	Edwin F. Corey, sr.	do	May 28 "	June 4 "
"	Edwin F. Corey, jr.	do	May 28 "	June 4 "
"	Thos. L. Thornell	do	May 31 "	June 5 "
"	Daniel Seixas	do	June 4 "	June 14 "
"	W. R. L. Ward	do	June 11 "	June 16 "
"	Henry H. Bostwick	Auburn,	July 31 "	Aug. 25 "
"	James W. Hale	New York city	Aug. 6 "	Not filed.
"	Henry C. Banks	do	Aug. 6 "	Aug. 12, 1858
"	Sylvester Lay	do	Aug. 9 "	Sep. 4 "
"	Lewis Hurst	Brooklyn	Aug. 9 "	Not filed.
"	William Birney	New York city	Aug. 12 "	Oct. 4, 1858
"	Henry Dunlap	do	Aug. 18 "	Sep. 15 "
"	Gordon L. Ford	Brooklyn	Sep. 9 "	Sep. 15 "
"	John M. McKinney	New York city	Sep. 11 "	May 19, 1859
"	James D. Hall	Brooklyn	Sep. 13 "	Not filed.
"	Solomon Dingee	New York city	Nov. 5 "	Mar. 12, 1859
"	Joseph G. Wilson	do	Nov. 22 "	Nov. 29, 1858
"	A. R. Woods	do	Nov. 22 "	Dec. 1 "
"	T. C. Callicot	do	Dec. 2 "	Dec. 10 "
"	F. E. Houghton	do	Dec. 27 "	Jan. 14, 1859
"	H. L. Emmons, jr.	do	Jan. 3, 1859	Jan. 10 "
"	Marcus D. Larrowe	do	Jan. 3 "	Not filed.
"	Thurber Bailey	do	Jan. 5 "	Jan. 17, 1859
"	Charles Nettleton	do	Jan. 5 "	Feb. 9 "
"	D. C. Osborne	Troy	Feb. 11 "	Not filed.
"	W. C. H. Waddell	New York city	Feb. 24 "	Mar. 7, 1859
"	Horace Andrews	do	Feb. 28 "	Mar. 4 "
"	H. P. Randolph	do	May 10 "	May 19 "
"	James C. Carlisle	do	May 12 "	Not filed.
"	Allan Rutherford	do	May 14 "	May 19, 1859
"	Edward Bissell	do	May 14 "	May 19 "
"	William Furniss	do	June 20 "	Not filed.
"	J. B. Nones,	do	Aug. 10 "	July 30, 1859
"	Fred'k Vincent, jr.	do	Aug. 4 "	Not filed.
"	Benjamin Rankin	do	Sept. 17 "	Sep. 23, 1859
"	John A. Corey	Saratoga Springs	Sept. 22 "	Not filed.
"	N. William Busteed	New York city	Oct. 13 "	Nov. 25, 1859

COMMISSIONERS OF DEEDS.

States, &c.	Names of Commissioners.	Residence.	Date of Appointment.	When evidence of Qualification filed.
New York,	John Livingston	New York city	Oct. 29, 1859	Not filed.
"	A. Van Sinderin	do	Nov. 12 "	Not filed.
"	Alex'r Ostrander	do	Nov. 30 "	Dec. 7, 1859
"	James E. Hadnett	do	Dec. 20 "	Not filed.
"	Francis A. Hall	do	Dec. 24 "	Dec. 28, 1859
Ohio,	Sam'l S. Carpenter	Cincinnati	Jan. 27, 1858	Feb. 4, 1858
"	E. A. Thompson	do	Jan. 30 "	Feb. 8 "
"	Alex'r H. McGuffey	do	Mar. 5 "	April 8 "
"	Edward R. Newhall	do	May 24 "	Aug. 12 "
"	Robert A. Folger	Starke county	May 28 "	Not filed.
"	John A. Lynch	Cincinnati	June 17 "	Sep. 30, 1858
"	James Parker, jr.	do	Sep. 15 "	Sep. 30 "
"	John G. Douglass	do	Dec. 22 "	Jan. 5, 1859
"	John P. Jackson	do	Oct. 12, 1859	Not filed.
"	John H. Piatt	do	Nov. 12 "	Nov. 22, 1859
Pennsylvania,	Jonathan H. Waters	Philadelphia	Jan. 11, 1858	Jan. 22, 1858
"	David H. Hazen	Pittsburg	Jan. 30 "	Feb. 5 "
"	J. P. Montgomery	Philadelphia	Mar. 31 "	Mar. 22 "
"	John Binns	do	Mar. 31 "	April 2 "
"	Arthur M. Burton	do	April 1 "	April 7 "
"	John H. Frick	do	April 1 "	April 21 "
"	Franklin Shippen	do	April 6 "	April 10 "
"	D. W. Hutchison	Erie	April 17 "	Aug. 9 "
"	Hugh W. Tener	Philadelphia	May 16 "	Not filed.
"	H. W. Safford	do	May 19 "	Resig'n rec'd July 10, 1858.
"	J. Wagner Jarmon	do	May 24 "	Sep. 9 "
"	Chas. E. Buck	do	June 28 "	July 12 "
"	Samuel Chew	do	Sep. 19 "	Sep. 27 "
"	David B. Birney	do	Aug. 9 "	Aug. 13 "
"	Benj. F. Blood	Pittsburg	Jan. 8, 1859	Jan. 20, 1859
"	Joshua Spring	Philadelphia	Feb. 14 "	Not filed.
"	Wm. Sergeant	do	Feb. 17 "	Not filed.
"	Samuel L. Clement	do	Mar. 11 "	Mar. 16, 1859
"	Charles Sergeant	do	Mar. 22 "	Mar. 31 "
"	Theodore D. Rand	do	April 16 "	April 21 "
"	John Binns	do	Sep. 24 "	Oct. 10 "
"	Edwin Smethurst	do	Nov. 2 "	Nov. 7 "
Rhode Island,	Wingate Hayes	Providence	Oct. 8, 1858	Not filed.
"	Henry Martin	do	Feb. 17, 1859	Feb. 24, 1859
S. Carolina,	Samuel J. Hull	Charleston	April 4, 1858	April 5, 1858
Tennessee,	J. D. Goff	Memphis	Mar. 17 "	Not filed.
"	Egbert A. Raworth	Nashville	Aug. 12 "	Aug. 12, 1858
"	T. W. King	Clarksville	Aug. 18 "	Not filed.
"	James E. Temple	Memphis	Feb. 7, 1859	Oct. 3, 1859
"	John H. Harrison	do	Feb. 14 "	Mar. 22 "
"	Edw'd B. Trezevant	do	Mar. 22 "	April 2 "
Texas,	J. Thompson Hallett	Austin	Jan. 29, 1858	Not filed.
"	E. F. Gray	Houston	April 17 "	Not filed.
"	Rob't D. Johnson	Galveston	April 26 "	May 21, 1858
"	A. F. James	do	June 8 "	Feb. 14, 1859
"	J. H. H. Woodward	Houston	July 13 "	Aug. 12, 1858
"	Wm. Anders	Harris county	Aug. 25 "	Sep. 22 "
"	Samuel Bell Maxey	Paris, Lamar co.	Mar. 11, 1859	June 27, 1859
"	Samuel J. Galbraith	Fannin county	May 26 "	Not filed.
"	John Reily	Houston	Nov. 15 "	Not filed.
Vermont,	Samuel Williams	Rutland, Rutd. co	Mar. 22 "	Not filed.
Wisconsin,	J. C. Starkweather	Milwaukie	April 6, 1858	Not filed.
"	Edward Pollock	Lancaster, Grant county	Aug. 5, 1859	Not filed.

TABLE

Showing the Times for the Commencement of the Regular Terms of each Circuit and Corporation Court.

Counties and Corporations	Circuit Courts. When terms commence.	County and Corporation Courts. Monthly terms.	County and Corporation Courts. Quarterly terms.			
	CIRCUITS.					
Accomack,	5. 1st Monday in May and 1st day of November,	Last Monday,	March,	May,	August,	Nov'r.
Albemarle,	10. 2d Monday in May and Oct'r,	First Monday,	Do	June,	do	do
Alexandria,	9. 3d Monday in May and 2d Monday in November,	Fourth Monday,	Feb'y,	May,	do	do
Alleghany,	14. 9th of April and September,	Third Monday,	March,	June,	do	do
Amelia,	2. 25th April and 20th October,	Fourth Monday,	Do	May,	do	do
Amherst,	10. 22d of March and August,	Third Monday,	Do	June,	do	do
Appomattox,	3. 21st April and September,	Thursday after 1st Monday,	Do	May	do	do
Augusta,	11. 1st June and 1st November,	Fourth Monday,	Do	do	do	October.
Barbour,	21.-8th May and October,	First Monday,	Do	June,	do	Novem.
Bath,	11. 15th May and October,	Second Monday,	Do	do	do	do
Bedford,	4. 25th April and September,	Fourth Monday,	Feb'y	May,	July,	do
Berkeley,	13. 24th April and September,	Second Monday,	March,	June,	August,	do
Boone,	15. 2d Monday after 4th Monday in April and September,	Wednesday after 2d Monday,	Do	do	do	do
Botetourt,	14. 26th May and October,	Second Monday,	Do	do	do	do
Braxton,	19. 27th April and September,	First Tuesday,	Do	do	do	do
Brooke,	20. 18th March and August,	Last Monday,	Feb'y	May,	July,	do
Brunswick,	2. 27th March and 2d October,	Fourth Monday,	March,	do	August,	do
Buckingham,	3. 5th April and September,	Second Monday,	Do	do	do	do
Cabell,	18. 27th March and August,	Fourth Monday,	Do	June,	do	do
Calhoun,	19. 12th April and September,	First Tuesday after 4th Monday,	Do	do	do	do
Campbell,	3. 18th May and October,	Second Monday,	Do	do	do	do
Caroline,	8. 1st March and 18th Sept.,	Second Monday,	Feb'y,	May,	do	do
			[To take effect June 1st, 1861.]			
Carroll,	16. Monday before last Monday in March and August,	First Monday,	March,	June,	August,	Nov'r.
Charles City,	6. 18th May and November,	Third Thursday,	Do	May,	do	do
Charlotte,	3. 25th March and August,	First Monday,	Do	June,	do	do
Chesterfield,	2. 7th May and 12 November,	Second Monday,	Do	do	do	do
Clarke,	13. 12th May and October,	Second Monday in June and 4th in other months,	Feb'y,	May,	July,	October.
Clay,	15. 1st April and September,	Second Monday,	March,	June,	Aug.	Nov'r.
Craig,	14. Tuesday after 1st Monday in March and August,	Fourth Monday,	Do	do	do	do
Culpeper,	10. 1st Monday June and Nov'r,	Third Monday,	Do	May,	do	do
Cumberland,	3. 5th March and August,	Fourth Monday,	Feb'y,	do	July,	October.
Danville,	4. 22d March and August,	Thursday after 2d Monday,	March,	June,	Aug.	Nov'r.
Dinwiddie,	2. 20th March and 26th Sept.,	Third Monday,	Do	May,	do	do
Doddridge,	19. 22d May and October,	Fourth Monday,	Do	June,	do	do
Elizabeth City,	6. 15th March and September,	Fourth Thursday,	Do	May,	do	do
Essex,	8. 25th April and 12th Nov.,	Third Monday,	Do	do	do	do
Fairfax,	9. 1st Monday June and Nov.,	Third Monday,	Do	June,	do	do
Fauquier,	9. Tuesday after 1st Monday in April and September,	Fourth Monday,	Do	May,	do	do
Fayette,	15. 7th June and November,	Thursday after 2d Tuesday,	Do	June,	do	do
Floyd,	16. 1st Monday April and Sept.	Thursday after 3d Monday,	Do	do	do	do
Fluvanna,	10. 10th April and September,	Fourth Monday,	Do	May,	do	do
Franklin,	4. 15th May and October,	First Monday,	Do	June,	do	do
Frederick,	13. 10th June and November,	Monday before 1st Tuesday,	Do	do	do	do
Fredericksburg,	– – – –	Second Thursday,	Do	do	Oct'r,	Dec'r.
Giles,	15. 20th May and October,	Second Monday,	Do	do	Aug't,	Nov'r.
Gilmer,	19. 19th April and September,	Tuesday after 3d Monday,	Feb'y,	do	do	do

7

TIMES AND PLACES OF COURTS.

Counties and Corporations	Circuit courts. When terms commence.	County and Corporation Courts Monthly terms.	County and Corporation Courts Quarterly terms.
	Circuits.		
Gloucester,	6. 13th April and October,	First Monday,	March, May, August, Novem.
Goochland,	10. 1st April and September,	Third Monday,	Do do do do
Grayson,	16. 4th Monday April and Sept.	Fourth Monday,	Feb'ry, do July, October.
Greenbrier,	14. 8th May and October,	Fourth Monday,	March, June, August, Novem.
Greene,	10. 3d Monday June and Nov'r,	Wednesday after 2d Monday,	Do do do do
Greenesville,	1. 28th April and 2d Nov'r,	First Monday,	Do May, do October.
Halifax,	3. 1st day of May and Oct.	Fourth Monday,	Do June, do Novem.
Hampshire,	13. 1st April and September,	Fourth Monday,	Do do do do
Hancock,	20. 10th March and August,	Tuesday after 2d Monday,	Jan'y, April, June, October.
Hanover,	8. 10th March and 26th Sept.	Fourth Tuesday,	Feb'y, do July, Novem.
Harrison,	21. 15th April and September,	First Monday,	March, June, August, do
Hardy,	12. 20th April and September,	Monday before 1st Tuesday,	Do do do do
Henrico,	6. 23d April and October,	First Monday,	Do May, do do
Henry,	4. 1st April and September,	Second Monday,	Do June, do do
Highland,	12. 2d May and October.	Thursday after 3d Monday,	Do May, do October.
Isle of Wight,	1. 16th May and 18th October,	First Monday,	Do June, do Novem.
Jackson,	18. 2d May and October,	Second Monday,	Feb'y, do do do
James City and Williamsburg,	6. 25th May and November,	Second Monday,	March, do do October.
Jefferson,	13. 20th May and October,	Second Monday in June and October, 3d in other months,	Do do do do
Kanawha,	18. 27th May and October,	Third Monday,	Feb'y, do do Novem.
King George,	8. 23d March and 12th Sept.	First Thursday,	March, do do do
King & Queen,	8. 2d May and 19th of Nov'r,	First Thursday,	Do May, do do
King William,	8. 13th May and 25th Nov'r,	Fourth Monday,	Do do do do
Lancaster,	8. 15th April and 2d Nov'r,	Third Monday,	Do do do do
Lee,	17. 2d Monday after 4th Monday in April and September,	— —	Do June, do do
Lewis,	19. 8th May and October,	Second Monday,	April, do do Septem.
Logan,	15. 1st Monday after 4th Monday in April and September,	Third Monday,	March, do do Novem.
Loudoun,	9. 4th Monday in April and 3d Monday in October,	Second Monday,	Do do do do
Louisa,	10. 20th April and September,	Second Monday,	Do do do do
Lunenburg,	2. 13th April and 8th October,	Second Monday,	Do May, do do
Lynchburg,	3. 3d of June and 3d Nov'r,	First Monday,	Do June, do October.
Madison,	10. 1st Monday March and Aug.	Fourth Thursday,	Feb'y, do do do
Marion,	21. 10th June and November,	First Monday,	March, do do Novem.
Marshall,	20. 1st May and 1st October,	Third Monday,	Do do de do
Matthews,	6. 6th April and September,	Second Monday,	Do May, do do
Mason,	18. 18th April and 18th Sept.	First Monday,	Feb'y, June, do do
Mecklenburg,	2. 2d of April and 15th Sept.	Third Monday,	Do May, do do
Mercer,	15. 27th May and October,	Thursday after 2d Monday,	March, June, do do
McDowell	17. 1st Monday March and Aug.	Second Monday,	Do do do do
Middlesex,	6. 1st April and October,	Fourth Wednesday,	Do May, do do
Monongalia,	20. 1st of April and September,	Fourth Monday,	Do June, do do
Monroe,	14. 25th April and September,	Third Monday,	Do do Sept. do
Montgomery,	16. 2d Monday in April and Sept.	First Monday,	Do do do do
Morgan,	13. 6th May and October,	Fourth Monday,	Do do Sept. do
Nansemond,	15. 16th April and 12th October,	Second Monday,	Do do August, do
Nelson,	10. 27th day of April and Sept.	Fourth Monday,	Feb'y, May, July, do
New Kent,	6. 10th May and November,	Second Thursday,	March, do August, do
Nicholas,	15. 6th April and September,	Monday before 2d Tuesday,	Do June, de do
Norfolk city,	1. 1st June and 15th November,	Fourth Monday,	Feb'y, April, July, October.
Norfolk county,	1. 1st April and 28th Sept.	Third Monday,	March, June, August, Novem.
Northampton,	5. 3d Monday in April and Sept.	Second Monday,	Do do Sept. do
Northumberland	8. 9th April and 28th October,	Second Monday,	Do May, August, do
Nottoway,	2. 20th April and 15th October,	First Thursday,	Do do do do
Ohio,	20. 10th May and October,	Second Monday,	Feb'y, July, Sept. Decem.
Orange,	10. 1st May and October,	Fourth Monday,	March, May, August, Novem.
Page,	12. 11th April and September,	Fourth Monday,	Feb'y, do July, do
Patrick,	4. 12th April and September,	Fourth Monday,	Do do do do
Pendleton,	12. 27th April and September,	Thursday after 1st Tuesday,	March, June, Sept. do
Petersburg,	2. 22d May, 16th November,	Third Thursday,	Do do do Decem.
Pittsylvania,	4. 28th May and October,	Third Monday,	Do do August, Novem.
Pleasants,	19. 30th May and October,	Thursday after 2d Monday,	Feb'y, May, July, October.

TIMES AND PLACES OF COURTS.

Counties and Corporations	Circuit Courts. When terms commence.	County and Corporation Courts. Monthly terms.	County and Corporation Courts Quarterly terms.
	CIRCUITS.		
Pocahontas,	14. 16th April and September,	First Tuesday,	March, June, August, Nov
Powhatan,	2. 2d May and 27th October,	First Wednesday,	Do do do Oct.
Preston,	21. 18th March and August,	Second Monday,	Feb'y, May, July, Nov.
Princess Anne,	1. 25th May and 22d September,	First Monday,	March, June, August, do
r nce Edward,	3. 15th March and August,	Third Monday,	Feb'y, May, July do
Prince George,	2. 17th May and 12th Nov.	Second Thursday,	March, do August, do
Prince William,	9. 2d Monday in May and Oct.	First Monday,	Do June, do do
Pulaski,	16. 3d Monday in April and Sept.	Thursday after 1st Monday,	Do do do do
Putnam,	18. 8th April and September,	Fourth Monday,	Do do do do
Raleigh,	15. 3d Monday April and Sept.	First Monday,	Do do do do
Randolph,	21. 26th May and October,	Fourth Monday,	Do do do do
Rappahannock,	9. 3d Monday in March and 1st Monday in October,	Second Monday,	Do May, do do
Richmond City,	7. 1st November and 1st May,	Second Monday,	Jan'y, April, July, Oct.
Richmond Co.,	8. 3d April and 23d October,	First Monday,	March, May, August, Nov.
Ritchie,	19. 15th April and September,	Tuesday after 1st Monday,	Feb'y, June, do do
Roane,	18. 17th May and October,	First Monday,	Jan'y April, July, Sept.
Roanoke,	14. Wednesday after 4th Monday in March and August,	Third Monday,	March, June, August, Nov.
Rockbridge,	11. 12th April and September,	Monday before 1st Tuesday,	Do do do do
Rockingham,	12. 11th May and October,	Third Monday,	Feb'y May, do do
Russell,	17. 4th Monday April and Sept.	Tuesday after 1st Monday,	March, June, do do
Scott,	17. 3d Monday after 4th Monday April and September,	Tuesday after 2d Monday,	Do do do do
Shenandoah,	12. 30th March and August,	Monday before 2d Tuesday,	Do do do do
Smyth,	17. 1st Monday April and Sept.	Tuesday after 1st Monday,	Do do do do
Southampton,	1. 2d May and 7th October,	Third Monday,	Do do do do
Spottsylvania,	8. 20th May and 6th October,	First Monday,	Do do do do
Stafford,	9. 4th Monday March and Sept.	Third Wednesday,	Do do do do
Staunton,	— — — —	Wednesday after 1st Monday,	Feb'y, May, July, Oct.
Surry,	1. 10th May and 25th October,	Fourth Monday,	March, do August, Nov.
Sussex,	1. 24th April and 29th October,	First Thursday,	Do do do Oct.
Taylor,	21. 4th March and August,	Fourth Monday,	Do June, do Nov.
Tazewell,	17. Last Monday March and Aug.	Wednesday after 1st Monday,	Feb'y, May, July, Oct.
Tucker,	21. 22d May and October,	Third Monday,	March, June, August, Nov.
Tyler,	20. 22d April and September,	Second Monday,	Do do do do
Upshur,	21. 4th April and September,	Third Monday,	Do do do do
Warren,	12. 25th March and August,	Third Monday,	Do May, do do
Warwick,	6. 21st March and September,	Second Monday,	Do June, do Dec.
Washington,	17. 2d Monday April and Sept.	Fourth Monday,	Do do do Nov.
Wayne,	18. 20th March and August,	Tuesday after 1st Monday,	Do do do do
Webster,	15. 14th April and September,	Fourth Tuesday,	do do do
Westmoreland,	8. 23d March and 18th Oct.	Fourth Monday,	April, May, do do
Wetzel,	20. 12th April and September,	Tuesday after 1st Monday,	Feb'y, do July, Oct.
Williamsburg,	6. 25th May and November,	Fourth Monday,	March, June, August, Nov.
Winchester,	— — — —	First Saturday,	Do May, do do
Wirt,	19. 3d April and September,	Tuesday after 4th Monday,	Feb'y, June, do do
Wise,	17. 1st Monday after 4th Monday in April and September,	Fourth Monday,	March, do do do
Wood,	19. 5th June and November,	Third Monday,	Feb'y, do do do
Wyoming,	15. 4th Monday April and Sept.	Friday after 3d Monday,	March, do do do
Wythe,	12. 1st Monday May and Oct.	Second Monday,	Do do do do
York,	6. 23th March and September,	Third Monday,	Do May, do Oct.

INDEX
TO THE ACTS OF THE GENERAL ASSEMBLY.

BERKELEY COUNTY.

An act giving the consent of the State of Virginia to the county of Berkeley being admitted into and becoming part of the state of West Virginia,... 41
Preamble,.. 41
Polls to be opened,................................. 41
Poll Books,... 41
Superintendence,.................................... 42
Form of returns,..................................... 42
Where said returns are to be filed,..... 42
Governor may postpone opening of polls,.. 42
When said county may become part of new state,.. 42
Commencement,...................................... 42

BIDDLE, SPENCER

An act authorizing the county court of Marshall county to re-assess two hundred and six acres of land in Marshall county belonging to,.......... 12
Proviso,.. 12
Commencement,...................................... 12

BOARD OF PUBLIC WORKS.

An act authorizing the board of public works to hire out certain convicts, 26
Preamble,.. 26
Commencement,...................................... 27

BRIDGES.

An act making an appropriation to rebuild a bridge over Stony river on the northwestern turnpike in Hardy county,.. 36
Commencement,...................................... 37

BROOKE ACADEMY.

An act to repeal and re-enact section second of an act to authorize the trustees of, to transfer their property to the Meade Collegiate Institute and to authorize said Institute to transfer the same property to the trustees hereinafter appointed, passed February 6, 1862,........................... 27

Section 2nd amended and re-enacted,.. 27
Commencement,...................................... 27

BUCKHANNON.

An act extending the boundary line of, 4
Commencement,...................................... 4

CAPITATION TAX.

An act appropriating the capitation tax for the year 1862, for educational purposes,................................. 37
The auditor to ascertain the amount paid into the treasury for the years 1861 and 1862,..................................... 27
How fund to be applied,...................... 37
What constitutes the fund,................. 37
Proviso,.. 37
Commencement,...................................... 37

CITIZENS' RAILWAY COMPANY.

An act to incorporate the citizens' railway company of the city of Wheeling,.. 33
Name of company,................................ 33
Powers,.. 33
Consent,... 33
Capital stock,... 34
Shares,... 34
Notice of meetings,............................... 34
Organization,... 34
Terms,.. 34
May increase capital stock,................. 34
Wheeling and Belmont Bridge Company may subscribe,......................... 34
Transfer of stock,.................................. 35
Dividends,... 35
Guage of road,....................................... 35
Offences,.. 35
Limitation of suit,................................ 35
Grades of streets,.................................. 36
Powers of corporations through which road passes,... 36
Tax,.. 36
Fare,... 36
Commencement,...................................... 36

CLARKSBURG COAL AND IRON COMPANY.

An act to incorporate,................

Name and style of company,............ 25
Capital stock,................................. 25
Shares,... 25
Subscriptions,................................. 25
President and directors may purchase land,... 25
Power to issue coupon or other bonds, 25
Commencement,............................. 25

COAL LANDS.

An act in relation to coterminous coal lands west of the Blue Ridge mountains in Virginia,........................... 11
No owner or tenant of land containing coal, permitted to open, sink, dig, excavate or work in any coal mine or shaft, within five feet of the line dividing said line from that of another, without consent in writing, 11
Penalty,... 11
Persons interested to have egress and ingress,.. 11
But not oftener than once a month,.... 11
Forfeiture for refusal,...................... 11
Summons,.. 12
Cost of summons, &c.,..................... 12
Commencement,.............................. 12

CODE.

An act to amend and re-enact section ten of chapter seventy of the Code, 22
Commencement,.............................. 23
An act to amend and re-enact the first and seventh sections of chapter forty-six of the Code,........................ 23
Commencement,.............................. 24
An act providing for the amendment and re-enactment of the eleventh section of chapter twenty-nine of the Code of 1860,................................. 28
Commencement,.............................. 28
An act to amend the second section of chapter four in relation to districting the State for representatives in congress,................................... 32
Section second amended and re-enacted,... 32
Apportionment of representatives,...... 32
Number of districts,......................... 32
First district,................................... 32
Second   "   32
Third   "   32
Fourth   "   32
Fifth   "   32
Sixth   "   32
Seventh   "   32
Eighth   "   32
Ninth   "   33
Tenth   "   33
Eleventh "   33
Commencement,.............................. 33

An act to amend and re-enact an act passed the 28th day of March, 1861, amending and re-enacting the seventh section of the one hundred and sixty-fifth chapter of the Code,....... 47
All acts or parts of acts inconsistent with this act repealed,................... 47
Commencement,.............................. 47
An act to amend and re-enact the second and third sections of the third chapter of the Code of 1860,.......... 67
Commencement,.............................. 68

COMMISSIONERS OF THE REVENUE.

An act authorizing the auditor to regulate the compensation of the commissioners of the revenue in certain cases,.. 69
Commencement,.............................. 70
When the auditor is required to appoint,.. 74
Commencement,.............................. 74
An act directing in what manner commissioners of the revenue in certain counties shall return their books,.... 66
Commencement,.............................. 67

CONN, CALEB

An act authorizing the county court of Preston county to re-assess one hundred and ninety and one-fourth acres of land in Preston county belonging to,..................................... 21
Proviso,... 21
Commencement,.............................. 21

CRIMINALS.

An act providing for the removal of criminals and criminal causes from the counties of Braxton and Randolph to the county of Lewis,......... 26
Commencement,.............................. 26
An act providing for the removal of criminal causes from the county of Tucker to the county of Preston,.... 29
Commencement,.............................. 29

CURRAN, PETER

An act to appropriate the residuary fund, under the last will and testament of,... 7
Appropriated to Brooke Academy,.... 7
Executors directed to pay to Brooke Academy,.. 8
Authority to sue,............................. 8
Power to sell,.................................. 8
Additional trustees,......................... 8
Commencement,.............................. 8

DAVIS, THEODORE

An act for the relief of,.................... 69

INDEX. 103

Released from fine, ... 69
Commencement, ... 69

‹ DEBTS.

An act to amend and re-enact the act passed July 26, 1861, entitled an act staying the collection of certain debts, 8
No writ of fieri facias to issue, ... 8
Levy, ... 8
Property to be returned to owner, ... 8
Lien, ... 8
Lien on real and personal estate, ... 9
What included, ... 9
Exceptions, ... 9
Commencement, ... 9
Expiration, ... 9
An act staying the collection of, ... 37
No writ of fieri facias or other process to issue, ... 37
No sales under any deed of trust heretofore executed, ... 38
Levy, ... 38
Property to be returned to owner, ... 38
Lien, ... 38
Lien on personal and real estate, ... 38
What is included, ... 38
Debtor required to pay interest on demand, ... 38
When creditor may enforce collection of his debt, ... 38
Proviso, ... 38
When debtor may contest creditor's right to proceed against him, ... 39
Proviso, ... 39
Exceptions, ... 39
Proviso, ... 39
Commencement, ... 39
Expiration, ... 39

DOGS.

An act imposing a tax on, ... 45
Proviso, ... 45
Housekeepers allowed one dog, ... 45
By whom taxes are to be paid, ... 45
Fine, ... 45
Number of dogs to be disclosed on oath, 45
How taxes collected and accounted for, 45
Duty of courts, ... 46
Lists, ... 46
Demand, ... 46
Duty of constables, ... 46
Fine, ... 46
Returns how to be made, ... 46
Fee for killing dogs, ... 46
How paid, ... 46
Fee for listing and furnishing copy of list, ... 46
How money arising from dogs disposed of, ... 46
Proviso, ... 47
Commencement, ... 47

DOWNEY, STEPHEN W.

Preamble, ... 10
Any court of this commonwealth, upon satisfactory evidence, authorized to grant a certificate of age, residence and character, ... 10
Commencement, ... 10

ELECTIONS.

An act changing the place of holding in the county of Preston, ... 9
The election heretofore authorized to be holden at Nine's house, in the eighth magisterial district, discontinued, ... 9
The election in said precinct to be held at the house of Wm. H. Brown, ,..... 10
Commencement, ... 10
An act changing the place of holding in the county of Jackson, ... 13
The election heretofore authorized to be holden at the house of William Slaven, in the fifth magisterial district, discontinued, ... 13
Commencement, ... 13
An act changing the place of holding in the county of Hardy, ... 17
The election heretofore held at Michael's abolished, ... 17
To be held at the house of John W. Athey, in Greenland, ... 17
An act changing the place of holding in the county of Monongalia, ... 17
The election precinct discontinued, ... 17
The election to be held at the house of James Arnett, ... 17
Commencement, ... 17
An act establishing a place of voting at Rockford school-house in the 3d magisterial district of Harrison county, ... 18
Commencement, ... 18
An act authorizing the governor to postpone the May election for the year 1863, ... 31
Commencement, ... 31

ELK RIVER.

An act declaring a part of, a lawful fence, ... 20
Commencement, ... 20

FISHER, GEORGE

An act for the relief of, commissioner of the revenue for Lewis county, ... 31
Auditor to pay seventy-five dollars, ... 31
Commencement, ... 31

FISHING CREEK.

An act declaring the north fork in the county of Wetzel, a public highway, 2 8

Unlawful to obstruct navigation of,......29
Commencement, ...29

FRANKLIN INSURANCE COMPANY.

An act to incorporate,........................ 4
Persons incorporated,...................... 4
Name of company,........................... 4
Rights, powers and privileges,............. 4
Rules, regulations and restrictions,...... 4
Capital stock,................................. 4
Value of shares,.............................. 4
Subjects of insurance,.- 4
Endowments,................................. 4
Reversionary payments,.................... 4
May guarantee payment of promissory notes, ... 5
May be insured,.............................. 5
May invest in stocks, &c.,................. 5
May loan money,............................. 5
May discount notes or bills of exchange, 5
Secretary a competent witness,........... 5
Proviso,....................................... 5
When the capital stock is payable,...... 5
Subscribers when to give bond,.......... 5
Condition of bond,.......................... 5
How interest and damages may be recovered against subscribers failing to pay,... 5
Who to examine bonds,..................... 5
May require new bonds,..................... 6
Failure to give bond,........................ 6
Officers, ... 6
Quorum,....................................... 6
Directors how elected,....................\.. 6
Terms of office of president, vice president and directors,........................ 6
Vacancy how filled,.......................... 6
How secretary appointed,.................. 6
Compensation,............................... 6
Agents,.. 6
Rules, orders and by-laws,................. 6
Scale of voting,.............................. 6
Who not permitted to transfer stock or receive dividends,........................ 7
Commissioners,.............................. 7
Notice,.. 7
Responsibility of stockholders,........... 7
Location of company,....................... 7
Commencement, ... 7
Perpetual,..................................... 7
Reservation,.................................. 7

GUYANDOTTE, BANK OF

An act to amend and re-enact an act entitled an act to incorporate the bank of Guyandotte, passed March 2, 1854,......................................75
Sections first, second, third and eighth amended,...................................75
Commencement, ...77

HARRISON, GREENVILLE

An act for the relief of,....................68
Auditor directed to issue his warrant in favor of,....................................68
Commencement, ...69

HAY, ALEXANDER

An act for the relief of,....................72
Sale of Alexandria and Washington railroad made a lawful sale,............72
Not affected by the law staying the collection of certain debts,.................73
Commencement, ...73

HILDRETH, SAMUEL P.

An act for the relief of, treasurer of the savings' bank of Wheeling,............12
Auditor directed to issue his warrant in favor of,....................................12
Commencement,...........................12

HOLLIDAY'S COVE RAILROAD COMPANY.

An act to amend the charter of,..........17
Permission,..................................17
Sections repealed,..........................17
Proviso,......................................17
Commencement, ...17

HOSTAGES.

An act authorizing the governor to arrest disloyal persons as hostages,......63
Preamble,....................................63
Who to be seized and held as hostages,63
Commencement, ...63

JACKSON COUNTY.

An act changing a place of voting in,...43
Commencement, ...43

KANAWHA BOARD.

An act to amend and re-enact the act passed May 15, 1862, entitled an act to re-organize the Kanawha board,...29
Section four amended and re-enacted,..30
Section five amended and re-enacted,...30
Commencement, ...30

KIMBALL, CHAS. H. (TRUSTEE,)

An act to authorize, to construct and maintain a tram or railroad from Franklin Furnace to the B. & O. R. R., in the county of Preston,............13
May be amended or repealed by general assembly,..................................13
Commencement, ...13

LEWIS, FERDINAND

An act to legalize the appointment of, as administrator of the estate of Solomon Michael, sr., late of Hardy county,.....................................30

Bond authorized to be filed in Preston county court,..30
Commencement, ...30

LITTLE KANAWHA NAVIGATION COMPANY.

An act to incorporate,............................70
Who authorized to open books of subscription,..70
Capital stock,..70
Name of company,..70
Number of votes authorized to be cast by stockholders,.....................................70
Improvements,..70
Tolls,..71
Power to borrow money,............................71
In what time improvements to be commenced,...71
Commencement, ...71

LUNATIC ASYLUM.

An act appropriating forty thousand dollars to the Lunatic Asylum west of the Allegheny mountains,............25
How to be expended,......................................25
Commencement, ...25

MAYO, E. H.

An act for the relief of,............................31
Commencement,...31

MARTINEY, JOSEPH

An act for the relief of, late commissioner of the revenue for Barbour county,..10
Auditor directed to issue his warrant in favor of,..10
Commencement,...10

MILITARY DUTY.

An act allowing certain claims out of any money derived from assessment of fines for the non-performance of military duty, under the order of the governor by his proclamation dated September 9, 1862,......................................40
Expenses of militia,......................................40
Commencement,...40

MILEAGE.

An act allowing to the delegates of the convention,..29
Commencement,...29

MISDEMEANORS.

An act repealing an act passed February 15, 1862, entitled an act to provide for the payment of costs in prosecutions for misdemeanors,......................75
Commencement, ...75

MORGAN COUNTY.

An act changing the place of holding elections in,...40
New place of voting,......................................40
Commencement, ...40

ORDINANCE.

An act to amend and re-enact the seventh section of the ordinance passed June 19, 1861, entitled an ordinance to authorize the apprehending of suspicious persons in time of war,........63
Commencement, ...63
An act amending and re-enacting the fourth section of the ordinance passed June 21, 1861,......................................73
Commencement, ...74

PARSONS, SOLOMON

An act for the relief of, in the county of Tucker,..43
Auditor to issue warrant,............................43
Commencement, ...43

PITTSBURGH AND STEUBENVILLE COAL COMPANY.

An act to incorporate,................................21
Style of company,...21
Subject to rules, regulations and restrictions of Code,...21
Shares,..21
Subscriptions,..21
Proportion of votes,......................................21
Directors,..22
Power of president and directors,........22
Authorized to construct a railroad,......22
May acquire not exceeding fifty acres of land,..22
Commencement, ...22

PLEASANTS COUNTY.

An act changing the place of holding elections in,...41
Election precinct abolished,......................41
Election precinct established,..................41
Commencement, ...41

PUBLIC HEALTH.

An act amending and re enacting section thirteen of an act passed July 26, 1861, entitled an act to provide for the public health,......................75
Commencement, ...75

PUBLIC REVENUE.

An act appropriating for the fiscal year 1862-3 and a part of the fiscal year 1863-4,..60
Expenses of general assembly,............61
Salaries of officers of civil government,.61
Judiciary,..61

Criminal charges,..................................61
Contingent expenses of courts,...........61
Convicts,...61
Lunatics,..61
Adjutant General,..............................61
Public printer,...................................61
Elections, ...61
Commissioners of revenue,.................61
Coroner's inquests,............................61
Clerks in auditor's office,...................61
Clerks in treasurer's office,.................61
Clerks in adjutant general's office,........61
Janitor,..61
Contingent expenses of auditor, treasurer and secretary of the commonwealth,.......................................61
Civil contingent fund,..........................61
Expenses of convention,....................61
Vaccine agent,..................................61
Principal of Linsley Institute,..............62
Sick, wounded and dead soldiers belonging to Virginia regiments,...........62
Sergeant-at-arms of house of delegates,62
Mrs. Tompkins,................................62
Collecting and taking care of arms,......62
Clerk of senate,................................62
Who not entitled to claim or receive any money by virtue of this act,.......62
What moneys to constitute a general fund,...62
Commencement, ...62

RED MEN.

An act to incorporate Logan Tribe, No. 21 of the improved order of, in the city of Wheeling,............................16
Individuals incorporated,....................16
Made a body politic and corporate,.......16
Name and style of company,..............16
Authorized to make all needful laws and regulations,..............................16
Commencement, ...16
May be altered, amended or repealed,_16

RATHBONE'S HEIRS

An act for the relief of Wm. P. Rathbone's heirs,................................47
Preamble, ...47
Commissioners,.................................47
Commissioners to make deeds,............47
Rathbone Petroleum company incorporated, ...48
Capital stock,...................................48
Authorized to use steam and other vessels and vehicles necessary for their business,...51
Commencement, ...51
May be altered, amended or repealed,..51

SLACK, JOHN JR.,

An act for the relief of,..................... 3

Allowed until the 20th day of February 1863, to give bond and security,........ 3
Commencement,............................... 3

SMITH & WILLIAMS.

An act authorizing, to sell goods in Jackson county,...... 24
Sheriff authorized to issue a license to,24
Proviso,..24
Commencement,................................24

SEVENTH CONGRESSIONAL DISTRICT.

An act providing for the return of the special election for a representative in, held on the 15th day of January, 1863, ...24
Clerk of county court authorized to make returns,.................................24
Commencement,................................24

SUITS.

An act authorizing the revival of certain suits depending in the courts of this commonwealth,..........................74
Suits not to abate or be dismissed,......74
Commencement,................................74

STOUT, J. W.

An act for the relief of, late commissioner of the revenue for Pleasants county,...10
Auditor directed to issue his warrant,..10
Commencement,................................10

SHERIFFS.

An act providing for the repeal of an act passed February 13, 1862, entitled an act to provide for the extension of time to execute writs of fieri facias on certain judgments,..............14
Commencement,................................14

SNIDER, HENRY

An act for the relief of,......................44
Released from fine,............................44
Commencement,................................44

TAXES.

An act imposing taxes for the support of the Government,..........................51
Taxes,..51
Amount of taxation on real property not exempt, ...51
Tax on personal property not exempt, and on monies and credits,..............51
Slaves, ...52
Free negroes,....................................52
White males,....................................52
Public bonds,....................................52
Dividends of savings institutions and insurance companies,..........................52
Incomes and fees,..............................52

INDEX.

Tax payable by officers of government to be deducted at the time of payment of salary, ...53
Toll bridges and ferries, ...53
Ordinaries and houses of public entertainment, ...53
Houses of private entertainment and public resort, ...53
Cook shops and eating houses, ...53
Bowling alleys, ...53
Billiard tables, ...53
Bagatelle tables, ...54
Livery stables, ...54
Distilleries, ...54
Merchants, ...54
Sale of liquors, ...54
License to sell liquors, ...55
Merchant tailors, lumber merchants and fuel dealers, ...55
Commission merchants, tobacco auctioneers or ship brokers, ...55
Auctioneers, ...55
Sample merchants, ...55
Patent rights, ...56
Patent medicines, ...56
Agents for renting houses, ...56
Agents for hiring negroes, ...56
Stallions and asses, ...56
Theatrical performances, ...56
Refreshments in theatres, ...56
Public rooms, ...57
Shows, ...57
Porter, ale or beer, ...57
Stock brokers, ...57
Bank note brokers, ...57
Foreign insurance companies, ...57
Physicians, dentists and lawyers, ...58
Daguerrean gallery, ...58
Express companies, ...58
Bank dividends, ...59
On suits, ...59
Seals, ...59
Wills and administrations, ...59
Deeds, ...59
Internal improvement companies, ...59
Sales of horses, mules, jennets, asses, cattle, sheep or hogs, ...60
Carriages and other vehicles, ...60
Sales of slaves, ...60
Commencement, ...60
An act amending and re-enacting section eight of an act passed Jan. 31, 1863, entitled "an act imposing taxes for the support of the government," ..73
Commencement, ...73

TENTH VIRGINIA REGIMENT VOL. INFANTRY.

An act to provide for the payment of certain volunteers in companies A and B of the 10th Va. regiment volunteer infantry for services rendered, not paid for, ...44

Auditor authorized to pay certain volunteers, ...44
Proviso, ...44
Commencement, ...45

TURNPIKES.

An act providing for placing a part of the Maryland and Ohio Turnpike under the supervision of the county court of Marion, ...66
Proviso, ...66
Commencement, ...66

WAGGENER, CHAS. B., TRUSTEE.

An act to authorize to sell certain property in Mason county, ...18
Preamble, ...18
Commencement, ...18

WEST VIRGINIA.

An act in reference to the troops raised within the boundaries of the proposed state of, ...40
Troops of West Virginia, ...41
Commencement, ...41
An act transferring to the proposed state of West Virginia, when the same shall become one of the United States, all this state's interest in property, unpaid and uncollected taxes, fines, forfeitures, penalties and judgments, in counties embraced within the boundaries of the proposed state aforesaid, ..64
What moneys to be paid into the treasury of West Virginia, ...65
Suits to be brought in the name of the state of, ...65
State of West Virginia to account with this state, ...65
Proviso, 65
Duty of officers of state, 65
Duty of governor, 66
Commencement, 66
An act making an appropriation to the proposed state of West Virginia when the same shall become one of the United States, ...68
Additional appropriations, ...68
Proviso, ...68
The act passed May 14, 1862, repealed, 68
Commencement, ...68
An act giving consent to the admission of certain counties into the new state of West Virginia upon certain conditions, ...71
Lawful for the voters of Tazewell, Bland, Giles and Craig to declare by their votes whether said counties shall be annexed to West Virginia, ...71
Also the counties of Buchanan, Wise, Russell, Scott and Lee, ...71

Also the counties of Alleghany, Bath and Highland,..................................72
Also the counties of Frederick and Jefferson,..72
Also the counties of Clarke, Loudoun, Fairfax, Alexandria and Prince William,..72
Also the counties of Shenandoah, Warren, Page and Rockingham,..............72
Polls to be opened,............................72
Consent,..72
Duty of governor,..............................72
When election to be held,.................72
Commencement,..................................72

WHEELING.

An act to amend the charter of,............ 3
Section five of the act passed March 11, 1836, amended and re-enacted,......... 3
Who entitled to vote at city elections,... 3
Proviso,.. 3
Commencement,.................................. 3
An act to declare that the council of the city of, shall consist of two boards or branches,..14
When consent of both branches required,14
Each branch the judge of the qualification and election of its own members,14
To make all needful rules and regulations for government,......................14
Which board called second branch,.......14
Its capacity unimpaired,......................14
Exception,..14
Of whom first branch shall consist,.......14
How elected,......................................15
Elections for first branch,..................15
How long to continue in office,..............15
One member of first branch to be chosen annually from each ward,..................15
Who eligible 15
Power to fill vacancies,......................15
Power of removal,..............................15
Proviso,..15
Who to preside at meetings of the first branch,..15

Chairman *pro tempore*,.........................15
Salaries,..15
Quorum,..15
Who to preside in second branch,.........15
Duty of presiding officer,......................15
President *pro tempore*,.........................15
How vacancy in office of mayor filled,...15
Exception,..15
Temporary absence of mayor,..............15
Appropriations of money, where to originate,..16
Power of council in reference to this act,16
Commencement,..................................16
An act to regulate the election of officers by the council of the city of Wheeling,43
All officers to be elected by joint ballot,43
Commencement,..................................43
An act to confer upon the president of the second branch of the council of the city of Wheeling the power to administer oaths,..............................44
Commencement,..................................44

WHEELING RAILROAD BRIDGE COMPANY.

An act to amend the charter of,............19
The first section of an act to incorporate, amended and re-enacted,..........19
By whom books of subscription may be opened,..19
Where,..19
Amount of stock,................................19
Name of company,..............................19
Fourth section amended and re-enacted,20
Lawful to establish rates of toll,..........20
Proviso, ...20
Transfer of passengers,......................20
Balt. & Ohio Railroad and C. O. Railroad to commence and terminate their trips at the city of Wheeling,............20
Fourteenth section repealed,..............20
Fifteenth section amended and re-enacted,..20
Sixteenth section repealed,..................20
Commencement,..................................20

Printed in Dunstable, United Kingdom

82202523R00067